No More Sheets

Devotional

NO MORE SHEETS

DEVOTIONAL

JUANITA BYNUM

PUBLISHING

NO MORE SHEETS DEVOTIONAL

Printed in the United States of America
ISBN: 1-56229-149-1

Pneuma Life Publishing
Post Office Box 885
Lanham, MD 20703

http://www.pneumalife.com

CONTENTS

INTRODUCTION

ON A COLLISION COURSE

While driving down the street contemplating what things I needed to do in order to complete this devotional writing, I had what potentially could have been a fatal accident. I was waiting at an intersection with my signal light on to make a left turn. Lost in thought, I looked up in horror to see a speeding car coming right at me. At impact, I threw up my arms to protect my face, my seatbelt engaged and my airbag exploded. My car went into a spin and was knocked completely from the street and into someone's front yard.

The first thing I thought was, "I have to get out of this car before it explodes." Somehow, by the grace of God I was able to get out and move a couple of yards from the car before I collapsed onto the ground and passed out. When I came to, my mother and some of my god sisters were standing over me. All I could feel was pain. I didn't know whether I was alive or dead. All I could say was, "Lord please help me. Don't let me die." That's where many of you are as you're reading this devotional. You have failed in your walk with the Lord and have accidentally, incidentally or intentionally yielded your members to works of unrighteousness:

Neither yield ye your members as instruments of unrighteousness unto sin: but yield yourselves unto God, as those that are alive from the dead, and your members as instruments of righteousness unto God. Romans 6:13

Shortly after the accident an ambulance and the paramedics arrived. The paramedics' first concern was to revive me and make certain all my vital signs were stable. When I finally arrived at the emergency room my condition was diagnosed as being traumatic. I was in a lot of pain. Lying there on my back in the emergency room I remember thinking, "Oh my God, my head is pounding, my stomach is aching, and my car is totaled." Traumatic definitely described what I was experiencing both physically and mentally.

I recite this incident because the accident was and is a type of prophetic symbolism expressing the traumatic condition of being bound by sexual sins and the pain and despair of living with the emotional scars that make one vulnerable and susceptible to such a lifestyle. At the time of the accident, I didn't have to repent for unrepented sin nor did I have time to recite a sinner's prayer. This is expressly why the Bible tells us that as believers in Christ to be ready.

See then that ye walk circumspectly, not as fools, but as wise, Redeeming the time, because the days are evil. Ephes. 5:15-16

But God said unto him, Thou fool, this night thy soul shall be required of thee: then whose shall those things be, which thou hast provided? Luke 12:20

Realizing the severity of my situation, the cry of my heart on that day was, "Lord, don't let me die." The despair I felt for my life is very relative to what we feel when we live a life of bondage to sexual sin. The frustration of falling time and time again causes our soul to weep and long for deliverance, wondering if it will ever truly come.

We are troubled on every side, yet not distressed; we are perplexed, but not in despair; Persecuted, but not forsaken; cast down, but not destroyed; Always bearing about in the body the dying of the Lord Jesus, that the life also of Jesus might be made manifest in our body. 2 Cor. 4:8-10

Even when deliverance does come, many times we find ourselves back in the same predicament, over and over again. But don't you give up, my brother or sister. He Who began a good work in you will carry it out.

Being confident of this very thing, that he which hath begun a good work in you will perform it until the day of Jesus Christ:
Philip. 1:6

While I was in the ambulance, the paramedics and attendants were working frantically to revive me. These people were well-experienced and trained to give me the aid that my body needed at the time. I thought my situation was fatal, but these people had experienced and observed these situations time and time again. Because they were familiar with this type of situation they were well able to correctly assess my condition and apply the procedures. And what the medics were not able or trained to do, the physicians at the hospital were more than capable, skilled and experienced to perform.

I, as a Christian believer, have experienced in a very realistic way what it is like to be a slave to sexual bondage and promiscuity. As a human being, I have felt and endured the pain and heartache of being rejected by someone whom I loved very much. As a ministry gift of God empowered by the Holy Spirit, equipped with the mind of Christ and sent to the Body of Christ I have been given the mandate to help others get victory over the same sins and bondage that once and still continue to try and defeat me.

I don't claim to have all the answers to whatever sins and problems that may be presently plaguing you. However, I do know that by the power of the Holy Spirit and the delivering and healing power of the great physician, Jesus the Christ, you willafter reading this devotional come closer to absolute victory in your sexuality.

My heartfelt prayer is that God would bless and keep you.

Now unto him that is able to keep you from falling, and to present you faultless before the presence of his glory with exceeding joy, to the only wise God our Savior, be glory and majesty, dominion and power, both now and ever. Amen. Jude 1:24-25

ENJOY THE JOURNEY!!!

STATE OF EMERGENCY

When I pray, you answer me and encourage me by giving me the strength I need. Psalms 138:3

When I arrived at the emergency entrance, before they would service me, I had to go through the admittance process. During this, I was asked a series of questions to determine my identity and my present and past place of residence. They also asked for information concerning my insurance provider. This was done to ensure that they would be compensated for their services.

The next series of questions were asked to ascertain my past and present state of health. The answers to these questions were extremely important. The information gathered was to be used to ensure that I was not misdiagnosed or given medication that would cause an allergic reaction or any other type of negative response. They asked if I have any major diseases. My response was, "None that I knew of."

I was asked if any particular diseases ran in my family. I answered, "To the best of my knowledge, only what I've listed." They made inquiries to determine if I had previously been involved in any other accidents that resulted in any type of bodily injury. And if so, did I require surgery or extended therapy?

Now, just examine that entire emergency room procedure as it relates to your spirit being. Your past and present state affect the health of your soul and spirit. Ungodly soul ties have placed your spirit man in it's own trauma.

No doubt your soul is in a spiritual crisis. Your situation is urgent, it's an emergency. Believe me, I understand that when you've been bound for so long, there comes a time when your soul cries out, "I can't take it anymore. I want out of this, if I'm to survive I must be set free and must be freed now. It's an emergency!

ADMIT YOUR WEAKNESS

Be not deceived; God is not mocked: for whatsoever a man soweth, that shall he also reap. For he that soweth to his flesh shall of the flesh reap corruption; but he that soweth to the Spirit shall of the Spirit reap life everlasting. Galatians 6:7-8

Know ye not that the unrighteous shall not inherit the kingdom of God? Be not deceived: neither fornicators, nor idolaters, nor adulterers, nor effeminate, nor abusers of themselves with mankind. 1 Cor. 6:9

The first step in any realistic attempt at solving problems is to first acknowledge that there is a problem. To deny that you have a problem only makes the problem that much worse. When you ignore the problem and continue on behaving as if it does not exist, you only deceive yourself. And when you become self-deceived—yet continuing to sow seeds into the works of the flesh–you give the devil and your flesh the opportunity to strengthen it's hold on you.

But he said to me, "My grace is sufficient for you, for my power is made perfect in weakness." Therefore I will boast all the more gladly about my weaknesses, so that Christ's power may rest on me. That is why, for Christ's sake, I delight in weaknesses, in insults, in hardships, in persecutions, in difficulties. For when I am weak, then I am strong. 2 Cor. 12:9-10 NIV

All Christians–regardless of how long we have been born again or how much Bible we know–are constantly dealing with some issue(s) that we are trying to conform unto the knowledge of Christ. This is exactly why the apostle Paul declares that we are to take up the cross of Christ and die daily.

To believe that we are somehow exempt from the weaknesses of the flesh or the presence of sin in our lives is to only be self-deceived. However, we can be assured that if we acknowledge our sin before the Lord, He is willing and able to forgive, cleanse and restore us.

If we claim to be without sin, we deceive ourselves and the truth is not in us. If we confess our sins, he is faithful and just and will forgive us our sins and purify us from all unrighteousness. 1 John 1:8-9

In order to be free, you must remove the masks. No longer can you comfortably engage in behavior which you know is ungodly. You must confess your faults and sins. Be honest and true, not only to yourself but to God. He will forgive you and put you in right standing with him. Examine your life today. Admit that you have weaknesses. The truth shall make you free.

And ye shall know the truth, and the truth shall make you free. John 8:32

IDENTIFY THE PROBLEM

I call to remembrance my song in the night: I commune with mine own heart: and my spirit made diligent search. Psalm 77:6

Search me, O God, and know my heart; test me and know my anxious thoughts. See if there is any offensive way in me, and lead me in the way everlasting.
Psalm 139:23-24 NIV

Just as the attendants at the hospital asked me a number of questions in an effort to determine my identity and the source of my injuries, so must you identify why and how you came to be in the state that you're in. In doing so, you are better able to apply an effective, long-lasting solution. This principle not only applies to sexual bondage and sins of the flesh, it also applies to many other areas in our Christian walk.

Many times in our lives, we encounter trials and tribulations that do not seem to make any sense or have any relationship to our present situation. We may find ourselves in situations or in relationships where we express hostility, remorse or any number of negative or inappropriate emotions and have no understanding as to why.

There are issues and unresolved conflicts that have taken place over the course of time that continue to affect the quality of our present lives. In many instances, these are things that have taken place when we were children or during our adolescent years. If this is the case, it is difficult to determine what the source of the problems are (unless we have had prior knowledge). My sister and brother, you can be assured that if you go to the Lord in prayer, with a sincere heart, He will reveal to you the source of the matter. This is one of the many great benefits of having the prayer language of the Holy Spirit (praying in tongues).

But if we hope for what we do not yet have, we wait for it patiently. In the same way, the Spirit helps us in our weakness. We do not know what we ought to pray for, but the Spirit himself intercedes for us with groans that words cannot express. And he who searches our hearts knows the mind of the Spirit, because the Spirit intercedes for the saints in accordance with God's will.
Romans 8:25-27 NIV

Call unto me, and I will answer thee, and shew thee great and mighty things, which thou knowest not.
Jeremiah 33:3

*Ask, and it shall be given you; seek, and ye shall find;
knock, and it shall be opened unto you. Matthew 7:7*

Today, my beloved, I want you to go before the Lord in
sincerity and ask Him to search your heart and see if there
be anything in you that's not like Him. Ask Him to reveal
to you the error of your ways. When He does, ask Him to
give you the strength and courage to confront your problems. Don't run from the challenge; embrace it and allow
the Lord to empower you with whatever is necessary to gain
complete deliverance. Ask the Lord what has happened in
your past to make you vulnerable presently. Ask the Lord.
He will answer. He loves you. He want's you to be free more
than you could ever imagine. In fact, the Lord wants you to
be free even more than you want to be free.

IDENTIFY YOURSELF

Nay, in all these things we are more than conquerors through him that loved us. Romans 8:36

Ye are of God, little children, and have overcome them: because greater is he that is in you, than he that is in the world. 1 John 4:4

And hath made us kings and priests unto God and his Father; to him be glory and dominion for ever and ever. Amen. Rev. 1:6

And hast made us unto our God kings and priests: and we shall reign on the earth. Rev. 5:10

But ye are a chosen generation, a royal priesthood, an holy nation, a peculiar people; that ye should shew forth the praises of him who hath called you out of darkness into his marvellous light. 1 Peter 2:9

The Scriptures you have just read declare what the Lord says about you. The master strategy of the devil is to get you to believe things about yourself that are absolutely contrary to what the Word of God says you are. God has called us royalty. But you say, "Prophetess my actions indicate otherwise." Well brothers and sisters, I did not ask you what you act like…I told you what God says you are.

The devil exhausts an enormous amount of energy tempting us to sin. Satan convinces us that a little sex here and now is okay. Then, when you finally yield to the temptation he beats you over the head with guilt, telling you how filthy and wicked you are. Well, my beloved, what I am about to say may go against your religious training, but that's okay—you'll get over it. Who and what you are has absolutely nothing to do with what you do; it has everything to do with what Christ has done. Please take note that I said it is based upon what Christ *has* (past tense) done.

Jesus has done all that He is going to do to give you victory in this life. He lives to make intercession for us. But, if we are going to live a victorious life here on planet earth, we must appropriate what He has already done. The only way to accomplish this is to die to the dictates and will of the flesh. We must walk in the newness of life that Christ has provided for us.

> *Forasmuch then as Christ hath suffered for us in the flesh, arm yourselves likewise with the same mind: for he that hath suffered in the flesh hath ceased from sin; That he no longer should live the rest of his time in the flesh to the lusts of men, but to the will of God.*
> *1 Peter 4:1-2*

Verbally confess what the Word says you are. You are the righteousness of God in Christ Jesus. By the Grace of God through faith in His Son, Jesus Christ, you have been justified; You are the apple of your Father God's eye. Get up off your backside and speak the Word of God over yourself. If you say it, through faith, by the grace of God you have it. Based on the words you say, you will have victory or defeat, bondage or freedom, wealth or poverty, sickness or health, holiness or perversion. Child of God, the choice is yours. Whatever you say is yours.

And Jesus answering saith unto them, Have faith in God. For verily I say unto you, That whosoever shall say unto this mountain, Be thou removed, and be thou cast into the sea; and shall not doubt in his heart, but shall believe that those things which he saith shall come to pass; he shall have whatsoever he saith. Therefore I say unto you, What things soever ye desire, when ye pray, believe that ye receive them, and ye shall have them. Mark 11:22-24

ASSURANCE

I lift up my eyes to the hills where does my help come from? My help comes from the Lord, the Maker of heaven and earth. He will not let your foot slip he who watches over you will not slumber; indeed, he who watches over Israel will neither slumber nor sleep. The Lord watches over you the Lord is your shade at your right hand; the sun will not harm you by day, nor the moon by night. The Lord will keep you from all harm he will watch over your life; the Lord will watch over your coming and going both now and forevermore.
Psalm 121:1-8 NIV

No insurance? No service. This is the rule of thumb for most national health care providers. It is wonderful to know that in order for us to receive the help of God, we don't have to provide proof of insurance. God has given us *assurance* in His Word that in the time of need, we can call unto Him and He will not reject us.

The troubling thing about living in sin is that because of sin consciousness, we become reluctant and sometimes afraid to cry out to God for help. When we are depressed and defeated, that is the time we need Him most. Don't be afraid to cry out to your Daddy. The Lord won't reject you. You might be saying, "But Prophetess, you couldn't even begin to imagine the bad, awful, wicked, even perverted things I've done." It doesn't matter what I or anybody else thinks about you and your situation, what matters is what God thinks. What matters is that He will never leave you nor forsake you. This is the Lord's response to your sin—regardless of what it is:

Come unto me, all ye that labour and are heavy laden, and I will give you rest. Take my yoke upon you, and learn of me; for I am meek and lowly in heart: and ye shall find rest unto your souls. Matthew 11:28-29

You may say, "But I've sinned against God." And the Lord says:

If we confess our sins, he is faithful and just to forgive us our sins, and to cleanse us from all unrighteousness.
1 John 1:9

"But Prophetess," you say, "I've fallen time and time again, and no matter how hard I try I continue to fall!" Beloved, be not dismayed, know that God is All you need. Be assured that with every temptation that comes your way God will provide you a way of escape.

There hath no temptation taken you but such as is common to man: but God is faithful, who will not suffer you to be tempted above that ye are able; but will with the temptation also make a way to escape, that ye may be able to bear it. 1 Cor. 10:13

God commands us as believers to be holy, for He is holy. I know that because of the decadence and corruption of our culture and society, we are constantly being overwhelmed and bombarded by many wicked and evil temptations. Living holy can become a very difficult mandate to fulfill. But know that your heavenly Father will not ask anything of you that He will not give the necessary provision to carry it out.

For it is God who works in you to will and to act according to his good purpose. Philip. 4:13 NIV

I can do all things through Christ which strengtheneth me. Philip. 4:13

Use the Scriptures above in your time of meditation today. Think on these words in relation to God giving you the strength, fortitude, patience and perseverance that is necessary to maintain deliverance and holiness in your life. Don't give up!

Overcoming Temptation

The thief cometh not, but for to steal, and to kill, and to destroy: I am come that they might have life, and that they might have it more abundantly. John 10:10

If we are to be victorious as believers we must quickly dispel the erroneously religious belief that God brings bad things upon us in an effort to teach us righteousness. This is not true.

Every good and perfect gift is from above, coming down from the Father of the heavenly lights, who does not change like shifting shadows. James 1:17

The Bible also tells us that "God is love". Now if you are a parent and you're reading this, allow me to ask you a question. Would you purposely burn your child in an effort to teach him or her not to play with fire? Of course you wouldn't–that would be child abuse. So why would you believe that God, whose very essence is love, would be the originator of harm against your person in an attempt to teach you righteousness? You have one enemy–the devil. Satan is the *enemy* of your soul. Jesus is the *bishop* of your soul. Do you see the difference?

This is not to say that God will not use the bad things you encounter in life to mold and conform you into the character of Christ; however, this is not to imply that God Himself brings evil things upon you to test your character.

> *When tempted, no one should say, "God is tempting me." For God cannot be tempted by evil, nor does he tempt anyone. James 1:13 NIV*

Scripture clearly informs us that when we are tempted of sin, it is a result of the lust that lies within ourselves. When lust is conceived, it brings forth sin.

> *But each one is tempted when, by his own evil desire, he is dragged away and enticed. Then, after desire has conceived, it gives birth to sin; and sin, when it is full-grown, gives birth to death. James 1:14-15 NIV*

> *Then was Jesus led up of the Spirit into the wilderness to be tempted of the devil. And when he had fasted forty days and forty nights, he was afterward an hungred. And when the tempter came to him, he said, If thou be the Son of God, command that these stones be made bread. Matthew 4:1-3*

It's time for the people of God to stop being so phony and get real. Look, we are not little E.T.'s walking around so sweet and nice that temptation does an about face as soon as we show up on the scene. Oh, I wish you could read my lips right now, "You are not exempt from temptation." Maybe you think that just because you got baptized when you were 6 years old, Satan "done got tired" of messing with you. Wrong! Or, perhaps you think that because you're in the five-fold ministry, you have some exclusive membership rights that nobody else knows about–including Jesus Himself. Wrong! The devil is not a respecter of persons. If temptation made it's way to Jesus, then, guess what? Temptation will "straight dis" your title, your gifts and calling! So, you all need to recognize that no matter what the opposition, no matter what you're faced with, God has made a way of escape each and every time–just for you. Did you get that? You Will ALWAYS Have A Way Out!

There hath no temptation taken you but such as is common to man: but God is faithful, who will not suffer you to be tempted above that ye are able; but will with the temptation also make a way to escape, that ye may be able to bear it. 1 Cor. 10:13

Take a look at this Scripture in The Living Bible:

But remember this–the wrong desires that come into your life aren't anything new and different. Many others have faced exactly the same problems before you. And no temptation is irresistible. You can trust God to keep the temptation from becoming so strong that you can't stand up against it, for he has promised this and will do what he says. He will show you how to escape temptation's power so that you can bear up patiently against it. 1 Cor. 10:13 TLB

When the Bible says that no temptation has taken you but such as is common to man–basically, what it's saying is there's nothing new under the sun, so get over it. As cute as he is or as fine as she may be, they ain't the new Wonder of the World. Don't deceive yourself into thinking that just because you want to do it, then you might as well go ahead and do it. That lie has got to die.

Blessed is the man that endureth temptation: for when he is tried, he shall receive the crown of life, which the Lord hath promised to them that love him. James 1:12

Stop beating yourself up just because you're faced with a temptation. Please understand that the temptation–in and of itself–is not what's wrong. Yielding to the temptation is wrong.

Neither yield ye your members as instruments of unrighteousness unto sin: but yield yourselves unto God, as those that are alive from the dead, and your members as instruments of righteousness unto God . . . Know ye not, that to whom ye yield yourselves servants to obey, his servants ye are to whom ye obey; whether of sin unto death, or of obedience unto righteousness? . . . I speak after the manner of men because of the infirmity of your flesh: for as ye have yielded your members servants to uncleanness and to iniquity unto iniquity; even so now yield your members servants to righteousness unto holiness. Romans 6:13,16,19

To overcome temptation, first of all, you need to make sure that your thought process is in line with God's Word. Then, fine-tune your sensitivity to the voice of the Lord.

Recognize and heed the caution signs that lead to your highway of disaster. When God shows you your way out, take it! You know right from wrong. Come on, let's be honest–you know that if Jesus was right there, you just wouldn't do or say certain things. Well, He is there "for he hath said, I will never leave thee, nor forsake thee" (Hebrews 13:5b).

What? know ye not that your body is the temple of the Holy Ghost which is in you, which ye have of God, and ye are not your own? 1 Cor. 6:19

WORSHIP

Then saith Jesus unto him, Get thee hence, Satan: for it is written, Thou shalt worship the Lord thy God, and him only shalt thou serve. Matthew 4:10

But the hour cometh, and now is, when the true worshippers shall worship the Father in spirit and in truth: for the Father seeketh such to worship him.
John 4:23

God is a Spirit: and they that worship him must worship him in spirit and in truth. John 4:24

When the medical attendants began their diagnostic test, the first task that they performed was to hook me up to an I-V pack containing a mineral solution. The medics informed me that as a result of the trauma my body experienced during the accident, harmful toxins had been released into my blood. Therefore, my blood system had to be strengthened before any blood could be drawn.

That liquid, flowing through the I-V pack, reminded me of the purging and purifying power of the Holy Spirit–flowing through the tube going down into my veins–bringing about the anointing of God into my body. Just as the tube in my arm was being utilized as a vehicle to transport life-sustaining, cleansing solutions into my body, so it is with worship. In times of great distress, inner pain, and frustration, worship becomes a vehicle whereby God–through the person of the Holy Spirit–brings life and strength to your inner man. Through the awareness of the presence of the Holy Spirit, I realized that goodness and mercy followed me to the hospital.

The purpose of the examination that the medics were conducting was to determine what was wrong with me. Worship accomplishes the same purpose. That I-V was spiritually symbolic of worship.

Worship is what transports you into the presence of God. The presence of God is what helps you to define who you are and Who God is. You realize the absolute frailty of your humanity when you are in midst of the presence of God. Your submission to God in worship exemplifies that He is Everything and, without Him, you are nothing.

Worship is a very powerful tool against the works of the flesh and an extremely powerful tool against demonic oppression, demonic influence, and demonic thoughts. When we enter into worship, in a very true sense, we lose sight of ourselves, our problems, and our flesh. Worship gives us an awareness of the strength, power, and glory of God. Worship is what opens us up not only to the power of God, but also the anointing of God.

The anointing of God is able to destroy the yokes of bondage and strongholds that are upon our lives. Worship takes us from being man-conscious, problem-conscious, and problem-driven to being totally God-centered. In worship, we become totally overwhelmed with the presence of God, and the reality of God. When we truly enter into worship in the Spirit, the Spirit of God literally drives out the hordes of the devil.

Worship also is a place where we become embraced with the purging power of the Holy Spirit of God. The Lord desires us to yield ourselves in worship. Jesus told the woman at the well that the Lord seeks those who worship Him in spirit and in truth. When we begin to worship God, we then make ourselves susceptible to the cleansing power of the Holy Spirit. Purging cleanses us from the works and affects of unrighteousness upon our lives.

If we look at the life of David, we see that the key to David's many successes in life was that he was able to yield himself on a consistent basis in worship to God. If we read the book of Psalms, we find that there were many times David worshiped God. David gave himself completely over to God in worship. It was worship that enabled David to defeat his enemies in the many battles he engaged in during his lifetime.

And hope maketh not ashamed; because the love of God is shed abroad in our hearts by the Holy Ghost which is given unto us. Romans 5:5

Worship is also the place where we experience the love of God in a very tangible way. This is why many times, when we enter into worship, we have an uncontrollable desire to weep before God, to cry before the Lord. In the presence of God, we become so saturated with his love–as it is expressed by His Spirit–that, at times, it becomes literally impossible to maintain our composure. His presence is infused with His love. His very essence is love.

Completely abandon yourself in worship. Wherever you are, stop right there and give Him the glory because when praises go up, His blessings will come down.

Dare to soar in worship to the Lord, God Almighty.

Fellowship With God

And Moses went up into the mount, and a cloud covered the mount. And the glory of the Lord abode upon mount Sinai, and the cloud covered it six days: and the seventh day he called unto Moses out of the midst of the cloud. And the sight of the glory of the Lord was like devouring fire on the top of the mount in the eyes of the children of Israel. And Moses went into the midst of the cloud, and gat him up into the mount: and Moses was in the mount forty days and forty nights. Exodus 24:15-18

And when the people saw that Moses delayed to come down out of the mount, the people gathered themselves together unto Aaron, and said unto him, Up, make us gods, which shall go before us; for as for this Moses, the man that brought us up out of the land of Egypt, we wot not what is become of him. Exodus 32:1

And the Lord said unto Moses, Go, get thee down.
Exodus 32:7a

Worship is the place where our fellowship with the Father is most exemplified and amplified. When Moses stole away from the people of God and went up mount Sinai to fellowship with the Lord, he become so overwhelmed and fascinated with the presence of God that he did not want to go back down and be with the people. God had to literally tell Moses to get back down the mountain and go see about the people.

Like Moses, King David would spend hours and hours at a time before the Lord. David was absolutely, unequivocally addicted to the presence of God. When David sinned with Bathsheba and was convicted of God by the prophet Nathan, he responded by crying out: "Lord, take not thy Holy Spirit from me." He did not beg not to be reprimanded or even punished. He just wanted to be sure that he could still fellowship with and be connected to God.

Cast me not away from thy presence; and take not thy holy spirit from me. Psalm 51:11

For I am persuaded, that neither death, nor life, nor angels, nor principalities, nor powers, nor things present, nor things to come, Nor height, nor depth, nor any other creature, shall be able to separate us from the love of God, which is in Christ Jesus our Lord.
                                        Romans 8:38

If you maintain regular fellowship with God through worship and prayer, you will be less likely to yield to the temptation of sin. You will enjoy His presence so much that you will not want anything to break that fellowship.

Today, make a decision to not allow anything to separate you from God. Whether it be sin, condemnation, a loved one, a friend, a habit, a job, a church, a responsibility, a lie, or a ministry, stay in fellowship with God. Meditate on the Scriptures above and stay in His presence.

PRAYER

Praying always with all prayer and supplication in the Spirit, and watching thereunto with all perseverance and supplication for all saints. Ephes. 6:18

Pray without ceasing. 1 Thes. 5:17

But ye, beloved, building up yourselves on your most holy faith, praying in the Holy Ghost. Jude 1:20

Prayer, in its most simple form, is communication. If we're going to be victorious over the works of the flesh, and over the power of the enemy, we must first submit ourselves to God. And prayer is the first step in submitting to God.

Submit yourselves therefore to God. Resist the devil, and he will flee from you. James 4:7

When we read the Gospel and study the life of Jesus, we find that one of the things that Jesus did the most was pray.

Many times, Jesus would pray all night. Prayer was an act of His submission to the will of God. Now, we understand that Jesus was all man *and* also all God. However, we have to understand that when Jesus walked the face of the earth, he relied upon the same source that you and I as believers must rely upon to give us the ability to combat the works of the devil–the power of the Holy Spirit. This is why Jesus was the perfect example for man. Jesus showed us what is necessary to live a victorious life here on earth. I am aware that Jesus was just as much God as He was man. When Jesus walked the face of the earth, however, he divested Himself of the power which he had in heaven.

> *Let this mind be in you, which was also in Christ Jesus: Who, being in the form of God, thought it not robbery to be equal with God: But made himself of no reputation, and took upon him the form of a servant, and was made in the likeness of men: And being found in fashion as a man, he humbled himself, and became obedient unto death, even the death of the cross. Wherefore God also hath highly exalted him, and given him a name which is above every name. Philip. 2:5-9*

Taking this under consideration and observing in the Gospels how often Jesus prayed, we can conclude that the power He exercised over the works of the enemy was a result of this constant communion with the Father. Prayer was Jesus' life line to the Father God.

Make a decision today to commit yourself to a lifestyle of prayer. Spend a certain amount of time with the Lord each day. You don't have to start out with a full hour. You can vow to start with just five minutes a day–but be faithful to that vow. Once you get in the presence of God, that time will fly by and you will have to take notice of the time. Be consistent.

I find that the morning is the best time of day to spend with God. Each day, you should not show your face to any man until you have first shown your face to God. Get in His presence and get His will for your day before the hectic pace and daily routine begin.

Sometimes, it is a press to get up, especially if you went to bed late or had a particularly trying day before. If you stay on track, however, you will cultivate a relationship with God that you never realized was possible. He will speak to you about every area of life. You will receive divine guidance and even begin to see things coming together in your life. The Lord will correct you, warn you, heal you, refresh you, speak to you, reveal Himself to you, and set your life on course. Start today.

SUBMISSION

Submit yourselves therefore to God. James 4:7a.

When I was being examined, if I would have interfered with the doctor while he was trying to examine me, I would have impeded progress. I had to make an intelligent decision to yield to his expertise. He knew what he was doing; I didn't. He's the one who paid thousands of dollars for his education; I didn't. He's the one who went to medical school for over a decade; I didn't.

Nay but, O man, who art thou that repliest against God? Shall the thing formed say to him that formed it, Why hast thou made me thus? Romans 9:20

The earth is the Lord's, and the fulness thereof; the world, and they that dwell therein. For he hath founded it upon the seas, and established it upon the floods. Who shall ascend into the hill of the Lord? or who shall stand in his holy place? He that hath clean hands, and a pure heart; who hath not lifted up his soul unto vanity, nor sworn deceitfully. He shall receive the blessing from the Lord, and righteousness from the God of his salvation. This is the generation of them that seek him, that seek thy face, O Jacob. Selah. Lift up your heads, O ye gates; and be ye lift up, ye everlasting doors; and the King of glory shall come in. Who is this King of glory? The Lord strong and mighty, the Lord mighty in battle. Lift up your heads, O ye gates; even lift them up, ye everlasting doors; and the King of glory shall come in. Who is this King of glory? The Lord of hosts, he is the King of glory. Selah. Psalm 24:1-10

Just as I submitted myself to the expertise of the doctor, so I must also submit myself before God in prayer and worship. Once I got that IV in my arm, I didn't want to leave the hospital. I wanted to lie there because I knew I needed treatment and I knew I was in good hands. So must we be before the presence of the Lord God.

The minute you recognize Him as being the Greater Power, then the examination of your heart can begin. Before the Great Physician, Jesus Christ, can heal us, we have to admit that we're helpless patients and are at His mercy. Yield yourself to His treatment and analysis.

Neither yield ye your members as instruments of unrighteousness unto sin: but yield yourselves unto God, as those that are alive from the dead, and your members as instruments of righteousness unto God. Know ye not, that to whom ye yield yourselves servants to obey, his servants ye are to whom ye obey; whether of sin unto death, or of obedience unto righteousness?

I speak after the manner of men because of the infirmity of your flesh: for as ye have yielded your members servants to uncleanness and to iniquity unto iniquity; even so now yield your members servants to righteousness unto holiness. Romans 6:13,16,19

Submit yourselves therefore to God. Resist the devil, and he will flee from you. James 4:7

GOD'S PURGING

Purge me with hyssop, and I shall be clean: wash me, and I shall be whiter than snow. Psalm 51:7

Iniquities prevail against me: as for our transgressions, thou shalt purge them away. Psalm 65:3

Help us, O God of our salvation, for the glory of thy name: and deliver us, and purge away our sins, for thy name's sake. Psalm 79:9

And he shall sit as a refiner and purifier of silver: and he shall purify the sons of Levi, and purge them as gold and silver, that they may offer unto the Lord an offering in righteousness. Malachi 3:3

How much more shall the blood of Christ, who through the eternal Spirit offered himself without spot to God, purge your conscience from dead works to serve the living God? Hebrews 9:14

The nurse told me that almost immediately, I would feel the need to urinate because the fluids would flush out my kidneys. Worship opens up the bowels of your spirit so that the Spirit of God can flush out that stubborn will, rebellion and everything that would stand against God's purging and purifying hand.

When I got up to use the restroom, I wanted to take the IV out. The nurse told me, "No, you can not take it out. You must push it with you to the restroom." Likewise, so it is when God is dealing with us. Purging is not a one-time event that happens in an instant. Purging of wrong habits, corrupt desires, and impure thoughts and emotions take as long as it takes for you to totally submit your will to the will of the Father. You didn't get into the condition you're in overnight, and it will take more than just an overnight purging for you to get out. I know it might have started with one night of sinful pleasure, but you know you didn't stop there. Most of us kept going back for more and more.

Today, stop whining and get on the altar of the Lord and die. Die to a will that is contrary to the will of God. Die to sin. Die to carnality. Die to bad habits. Deliverance is sometimes immediate, but sanctification is an ongoing, continual process. This is why it is so important for worship to be a lifestyle, not just something you do in church. Wake up tomorrow morning worshiping God and go to bed tonight with His praises on your lips–thanking God that He let you live on His earth another day.

THE BLOOD OF JESUS

But if we walk in the light, as he is in the light, we have fellowship one with another, and the blood of Jesus Christ his Son cleanseth us from all sin. 1 John 1:7

Having therefore, brethren, boldness to enter into the holiest by the blood of Jesus, by a new and living way, which he hath consecrated for us, through the veil, that is to say, his flesh. Hebrews 10:19-20

Next was the drawing of blood so that they could examine it in the lab to make sure there was no presence of impurity or diseases. While they were checking my blood, I wasn't concerned. I knew I had been bought with a price through the blood of Jesus Christ. I knew that although I was in an accident and my body had been traumatized, the blood of Jesus was still covering me.

And they shall take of the blood, and strike it on the two side posts and on the upper door post of the houses,

wherein they shall eat it. For I will pass through the land of Egypt this night, and will smite all the firstborn in the land of Egypt, both man and beast; and against all the gods of Egypt I will execute judgment: I am the Lord. And the blood shall be to you for a token upon the houses where ye are: and when I see the blood, I will pass over you, and the plague shall not be upon you to destroy you, when I smite the land of Egypt.
Exodus 12:7, 12-13

Apply the blood of Jesus to your life today. Recognize that His blood has been shed for your salvation, purification, and deliverance. Just as the children of Israel had to apply the blood of the passover lamb to their door posts, apply the blood of Jesus, the spotless Lamb, to the door posts of your heart. The death that comes from sin and transgression will have to pass over your life.

APPLY THE WORD

*In the beginning God created the heaven and the earth.
And the earth was without form, and void; and darkness
was upon the face of the deep. And the Spirit of God
moved upon the face of the waters. And God said, Let
there be light: and there was light. Genesis 1:1-3*

As we observe Genesis, we see that the Lord begins the
work of creation by acknowledging that there is a problem,
identifying the problem, and solving the problem by the
appropriate application of His Word.

*In the beginning was the Word, and the Word was with
God, and the Word was God. The same was in the
beginning with God. All things were made by him; and
without him was not any thing made that was made. In
him was life; and the life was the light of men.*
John 1:1-4

As believers in Christ we must realize that we cannot live victorious lives apart from the continuous hearing, reading, meditating and application of God's spoken and written Word. The Word of God not only has the power to deliver us as it is breathed on by the power of the Holy Spirit, but the Word of God–hidden in our hearts–is the only source that can sustain us in the face of continued and future temptation.

Thy word have I hid in mine heart, that I might not sin against thee. Psalm 119:11

Today, memorize this Scripture. Make a commitment to meditate on this Scripture until its principle becomes real in your life. Meditate on this Scripture realizing that if you stay in fellowship with God and His Word, you will not sin against Him or His Word. Hiding the Word in your heart is a decision. Not committing acts that are contrary to the Word of God is also a decision. Therefore, it will be easier to decide now than to decide in the face of temptation.

MOVE FORWARD

Brethren, I count not myself to have apprehended: but this one thing I do, forgetting those things which are behind, and reaching forth unto those things which are before, I press toward the mark for the prize of the high calling of God in Christ Jesus. Philip. 3:13-14

Being a slave to any type of negative addiction—drug addiction, sexual addiction, food addiction, alcohol addiction, work-aholism, the need to buy things, fitness addiction—can be a very frustrating ordeal. If you have any addiction—other than being addicted to the presence of God—it becomes very discouraging to walk in victory for weeks, months, or even years only to find yourself falling all over again and again.

When one is bound by the power of destructive addictions, there actually comes a point in time where one becomes so overcome with despair that succumbing to the addiction appears to be the most viable option. When you think about the many countless times you've fallen in the past, it becomes very easy to consider completely giving up the fight. You think, "I've tried so many times in the past and failed, what's the use!" Beloved, I don't care if you have failed a thousand times in the past, KEEP GETTING UP!

For a just man falleth seven times, and riseth up again: but the wicked shall fall into mischief. Proverbs 24:16

Never dwell on the past, whether it be the victories or the defeats. Remember, the battle is not over until you win. And even then, know that the battle is not over. When you submitted your life to Christ you were immediately inducted into an army—the Army of the Lord. You are at war against the enemy of your soul until the day you disrobe your mortal body and take on immortality. Until that takes place, be advised that there are no peace treaties where the devil is concerned. He will never call a truce or retreat from his plan to alienate the children of God from their heavenly Father. However, you can defeat him in the various areas of your life in which he either has a stronghold or is attempting to place one.

Meditate on the above Scriptures. Forgive yourself and the others that hurt you. Let the past stay in the past. Learn from your past mistakes, but be encouraged that you have the power to overcome them. Look forward to your glorious future.

Onward, Christian Soldier!

GENERATIONAL STRONGHOLDS

Thou shalt not bow down thyself to them, nor serve them: for I the Lord thy God am a jealous God, visiting the iniquity of the fathers upon the children unto the third and fourth generation of them that hate me.

Exodus 20:5

Many have referred to this as generational curses and, to a degree, that is somewhat correct. However, a more accurate description of this would be generational strongholds that open the door to demonic spirits which continue to weld their influence from generation to generation. For example, a father who indulges in pornography may inadvertently cause his children to be exposed to it. If this happens—and this is not dealt with through the Spirit by a faith-filled believer—that demonic spirit will continue to manifest its influence from generation to generation—many times without ever being detected.

These types of spiritual strongholds are not only manifested in sexual characteristics, they are also manifested in many other areas of life. Poverty, divorce, sickness, strife and even murder are many times conveyed from generation to generation.

If you know that certain dysfunctional personality traits exist in your family–and they seem to pass from generation to generation–renounce those spirits and their influence. Reverse the curse and decree that godly heritage begins with you and your offspring. Meditate on the Scriptures below. Accept the character traits of your Heavenly Father. Determine to pass His character down to your children.

The boundary lines have fallen for me in pleasant places; surely I have a delightful inheritance.
Psalm 16:6 NIV

Know therefore that the Lord your God is God; he is the faithful God, keeping his covenant of love to a thousand generations of those who love him and keep his commands. Deut. 7:9 NIV

SEDUCING SPIRITS

Now the Spirit speaketh expressly, that in the latter times some shall depart from the faith, giving heed to seducing spirits, and doctrines of devils. 1 Tim. 4:1

Seducing spirits are among the most deceptive and misleading spirits that exist. Why do I say this? Because in most instances, the person who is being used by the evil spirit is unaware that this spirit is operating in their life. Seducing spirits usually attach themselves to people, who for some reason or another, suffer from a low self-esteem. More often than not, low self-esteem becomes existent in a person's life when that person feels rejected by someone whom they loved a great deal or held in high regard. This could be a parent, a spouse—one you are married to or divorced from—a girlfriend, or boyfriend.

The seducing spirit, realizing the person's need for acceptance, perverts that need and causes the person to project themselves and act in ways that warrant others' attention, especially the opposite sex.

Be not deceived: evil communications corrupt good manners. Awake to righteousness, and sin not; for some have not the knowledge of God: I speak this to your shame. 1 Cor. 15:33-35

If you discern that you are under the influence of a seducing spirit, rebuke that spirit and decree that you will awake to righteousness and not sin.

Soul Ties

This I say then, Walk in the Spirit, and ye shall not fulfil the lust of the flesh. For the flesh lusteth against the Spirit, and the Spirit against the flesh: and these are contrary the one to the other: so that ye cannot do the things that ye would. But if ye be led of the Spirit, ye are not under the law. Now the works of the flesh are manifest, which are these; Adultery, fornication, uncleanness, lasciviousness, Idolatry, witchcraft, hatred, variance, emulations, wrath, strife, seditions, heresies, envyings, murders, drunkenness, revellings, and such like: of the which I tell you before, as I have also told you in time past, that they which do such things shall not inherit the kingdom of God. But the fruit of the Spirit is love, joy, peace, longsuffering, gentleness, goodness, faith, meekness, temperance: against such there is no law. And they that are Christ's have crucified the flesh with the affections and lusts. If we live in the Spirit, let us also walk in the Spirit. Galatians 5:16-25

To understand soul ties, it is imperative to understand the characteristics of the soul. The soul is the part of man that is composed of the mind, will and emotions. Contrary to popular belief, it is possible to be spiritually born-again and yet be very fleshly. This is usually the result of an under-developed and non-cultivated soul. The soul is the middle entity between the flesh and the spirit. If your soul is not strengthened by the renewing of your mind and emotions, and is not subdued to the control of your spirit man, you are what the apostle Paul refers to a carnal believer:

For ye are yet carnal: for whereas there is among you envying, and strife, and divisions, are ye not carnal, and walk as men? 1 Cor. 3:3

For though we walk in the flesh, we do not war after the flesh: (For the weapons of our warfare are not carnal, but mighty through God to the pulling down of strong holds;) Casting down imaginations, and every high thing that exalteth itself against the knowledge of God, and bringing into captivity every thought to the obedience of Christ. 2 Cor. 10:3-5

One of the most powerful soul-ties is effected by sexual intercourse.

Do you not know that he who unites himself with a prostitute is one with her in body? For it is said, "The two will become one flesh" But he who unites himself with the Lord is one with him in spirit. Flee from sexual immorality. All other sins a man commits are outside his body, but he who sins sexually sins against his own body. Do you not know that your body is a temple of the Holy Spirit, who is in you, whom you have received from God? You are not your own; you were bought at a price. Therefore honor God with your body. 1 Cor. 6:16-20 NIV

When you engage in sexual intercourse with someone, your souls become entwined. I'll rephrase that: When you lie with someone other than your God-given spouse, you take on the soul of that person. This means that your emotions as well as your thoughts take on the will of that other person.

Sexual intimacy is not the only way that you can develop soul ties with a person. Close association with someone can also develop soul ties.

Do not be misled: "Bad company corrupts good character." 1 Cor. 15:33 NIV

This type of ungodly close association is how many homosexual and lesbian relationships are developed, even in the church. For instance, during a time of great vulnerability, a woman who may never have even considered a gay relationship, may become closely associated with another female—one who is very controlling and manipulative. Unfortunately, the end result is many times an illicit lesbian affair.

Another clear indication that a soul-tie still exists is when you still feel attached to someone you had been involved with. This means that you are not spiritually single yet. One way that people keep themselves in bondage to their past is by continually reliving scenes over and over again in their mind or creating delusional fantasies about their future. Face it, there are things all over the place that can remind you of an ex–a favorite restaurant, cologne or perfume, car, TV show, etc.–but you have got to stop prolonging your past and cut the tie that binds you to that soul.

Don't misunderstand me. There are intimate relationships that God ordains. I don't mean intimacy in the sexual sense, but intimacy that is characterized by familiarity coupled with mutual respect, confidentiality and honor. These types of relationships, governed by the Lord, can become a great source of blessing in our lives. They provide us with accountability. These friend have earned the right, through proven love, to speak into our lives. They provide reproof and rebuke as well as encouragement.

> *And it came to pass, when he had made an end of speaking unto Saul, that the soul of Jonathan was knit with the soul of David, and Jonathan loved him as his own soul. And Saul took him that day, and would let him go no more home to his father's house. Then Jonathan and David made a covenant, because he loved him as his own soul. And Jonathan stripped himself of the robe that was upon him, and gave it to David, and his garments, even to his sword, and to his bow, and to his girdle. 1 Samuel 18:1-4*

Renounce and break all ungodly soul-ties and commit to develop godly friendships with members of the body of Christ. You should encourage each other and pray for each other. Today, ask the Lord to remove people from your life who subtract from your life and bring people in your life who will only add to your life. Also ask the Lord to increase your level of discernment so that you will recognize those who the enemy is using to distract and discourage you.

Iron sharpeneth iron; so a man sharpeneth the countenance of his friend. Proverbs 27:17

LUST

Who being past feeling have given themselves over unto lasciviousness, to work all uncleanness with greediness.
Ephes. 4:19

Mortify therefore your members which are upon the earth; fornication, uncleanness, inordinate affection, evil concupiscence, and covetousness, which is idolatry.
Col. 3:5

Lust is an insatiable spirit and an unappeasable work of the flesh. Beloved understand this, lust can never be fulfilled. When we think of lust we usually think only in terms of sex. But lust is basically an inordinate affection for anything. One can have an uncontrollable desire for food, money, things, men, women, drugs, alcohol, cigarettes, the list goes on and on. Lust is lust, and once you give yourself over to it, it has the power to absolutely destroy your life. Lust is the foundation upon which most modern day idols are built upon. For whatever you lust after is what becomes your god. What you lust after is what occupies your attention and your time. What you lust after is where you deposit your strength.

Submit yourselves therefore to God. Resist the devil, and he will flee from you. James 4:7

Flee youthful lusts: but follow righteouness, faith, charity, peace, with them that call on the Lord out of a pure heart. 2 Tim. 2:22

Meditate on the Scriptures above. They will give you the faith you need to never use this phrase: "The devil made me do it." Replace lustful thoughts with thoughts of righteousness, faith, charity and peace. If lust begins to plague your thoughts, call a sister or brother who calls on the Lord out of a pure heart. Pray together. Encourage each other to submit yourselves to God. The Word promises that in so doing, the enemy will flee.

PORNOGRAPHY

I made a covenant with my eyes not to look lustfully at a girl. Job 31:1 NIV

Finally, brothers, whatever is true, whatever is noble, whatever is right, whatever is pure, whatever is lovely, whatever is admirable–if anything is excellent or praiseworthy–think about such things. Philip. 4:8 NIV

Don't let anyone look down on you because you are young, but set an example for the believers in speech, in life, in love, in faith and in purity. 1 Tim. 4:12 NIV

They are the kind who worm their way into homes and gain control over weak-willed women, who are loaded down with sins and are swayed by all kinds of evil desires. 2 Tim. 3:6 NIV

To the pure, all things are pure, but to those who are corrupted and do not believe, nothing is pure. In fact, both their minds and consciences are corrupted. They claim to know God, but by their actions they deny him. They are detestable, disobedient and unfit for doing anything good. Titus 1:15-16 NIV

For the grace of God that brings salvation has appeared to all men. It teaches us to say "No" to ungodliness and worldly passions, and to live self-controlled, upright and godly lives in this present age, while we wait for the blessed hope–the glorious appearing of our great God and Savior, Jesus Christ,

Titus 2:11-13 NIV

I know what you are saying, "Why did you have to go there?" Well, you knew it was coming. Pornography, like homosexuality, is an issue that is usually only mentioned briefly in the church. This is a very tragic indictment on the church because many members of the body of Christ are the victims of the effects of pornography in various degrees–either directly or indirectly.

The word pornography is derived from two Greek words: *Porno*, which means whore, and *graphia*, which means to write or depict. Pornography literally means "depictions of the activities of whores."

Pornography is any material written or visual, that is intended for sexual pleasure. Most times it is full of inordinate sexual images. This creates a hunger for unnatural acts which bring us into deep bondage to perversion.

Now that you are aware of what pornography is, it should not be to difficult to understand how pornography, like fornication, is both destructive and sinful.

If you have ever been involved in pornography, repent and ask the Lord to cleanse you. You may never have read actual pornography, but you may have a problem looking at members of the opposite sex without undressing them with your eyes or wondering what they would be like in bed. This is a strong lust of the eyes and should be dealt with as well. It may have been a movie–R-rated, not even X-rated–that inspired a strong imagination that has taken a hold of you.

Meditate on the Scriptures above and make a covenant with the Lord not to look at anyone lustfully or ever set your eyes on pornographic material.

MASTURBATION

Flee from sexual immorality. All other sins a man commits are outside his body, but he who sins sexually sins against his own body. 1 Cor. 6:18

I define masturbation as a bait that the devil uses to master you. How does this sin get entrenched in a person's life? The most common way is to get involved with someone who is not God's will for your life. The ungodly acts you did together are engraved on your mind.

Now the mere memory entices you to indulge your flesh. It controls you constantly, even without the person being present. Satan laughs at this. He says, "I got you so hooked that I no longer need somebody to bring you down. I can send you to hell with the spirit of your own mind. I can cause you death by your own hands."

When many Christians are asked the question of whether or not masturbation is a sin or against the will of God, they are usually hard-pressed to find a direct Scripture reference prohibiting its practice. In response to that, I have a question. Is it possible for one to pleasurably engage in masturbation without the aid of pornographic material or without dwelling on imaginations that are contrary to the Word of God? The answer is absolutely not!

And if thy right hand offend thee, cut it off, and cast it from thee: for it is profitable for thee that one of thy members should perish, and not that thy whole body should be cast into hell. Matthew 5:30

Now, read that Scripture again. If you were bound by masturbation and you heard Jesus preach that day, what would you think? In my opinion, Jesus made Himself very clear. Masturbation is sin, and it needs to be dealt with radically.

Many people feel that masturbation is just a physical release. But something happens in the spirit of your mind. When you travel into the thought realm to such a depth that your body is aroused, you have tampered with demons. You have left the reality of today and transcended out of the natural and into the spiritual. If that spiritual realm is not God's realm, you have just exposed your spirit to a satanic realm that has more to offer than just a sensation.

When you masturbate, you're actually allowing a spirit to arouse you. At the point of climax, you are out of control. Your spirit is wide open, and you don't know what spirit of perversion has jumped inside you. While you're operating in demonic activity through masturbation, there is nothing safe about it.

Once the act is finished, only your flesh has been satisfied. Whether you dwelt on thoughts of the past or went into the fantasy land of the future, the enemy has just expanded his corruption of your mind. If you are a virgin and you masturbate, you have also opened yourself up to be plagued by a sexual drive that is out of control–even if that drive is subconscious. The enemy will not stop tempting you until your fantasy becomes a reality. This is why we must be renewed in the spirit of our mind.

> *And be not conformed to this world: but be ye transformed by the renewing of your mind, that ye may prove what is that good, and acceptable, and perfect, will of God. Romans 12:2*

> *Casting down imaginations, and every high thing that exalteth itself against the knowledge of God, and bringing into captivity every thought to the obedience of Christ. 2 Cor. 10:5*

> *Let this mind be in you, which was also in Christ Jesus. Philip. 2:5*

We must make sure that our thoughts line up with who Christ says we are. First of all, repent. Then, take those ungodly imaginations and thoughts and say, "Satan, I rebuke you in Jesus' name. I cast this thing out of my mind. I am operating with a pure mind and pure thoughts. According to the Word of God, I am going to let Christ's mind be in me."

BREAKING STRONGHOLDS

For though we walk in the flesh, we do not war after the flesh: (For the weapons of our warfare are not carnal, but mighty through God to the pulling down of strong holds;) Casting down imaginations, and every high thing that exalteth itself against the knowledge of God, and bringing into captivity every thought to the obedience of Christ; And having in a readiness to revenge all disobedience, when your obedience is fulfilled. 2 Cor. 10:3-6

For though we walk in the flesh, we do not war after the flesh. One of the first principles in spiritual warfare is to first understand that even though we do have to combat the works of the flesh, spiritual warfare is not carried out through the flesh. Taking authority over demonic thoughts that are conveyed by Satan is not a mental exercise, it is a spiritual work. We must rely upon spiritual principles and we must rely upon the person of the Holy Spirit to work in and through us to accomplish this.

> *For we wrestle not against flesh and blood, but against principalities, against powers, against the rulers of the darkness of this world, against spiritual wickedness in high places. Ephes. 6:12*

The Word of God says that we wrestle not against flesh and blood–that also means our own flesh and blood. We cannot carry out spiritual warfare by the agency of the flesh. It must be done by the power of the Holy Spirit, through the authority of the Word of God.

> *"For the weapons of our warfare are not carnal but mighty through God to the pulling down of strongholds..."*

We see here that Paul reiterates what he has already spoken in the previous verse. For the weapons of our warfare are not carnal, they are not physical, but they are mighty through Who? God! Not through ourselves, not in our own ability, but through God. Not through just a mental ascension or memorization of Scripture, but Scripture applied by and through the person of the Holy Spirit. The Word of God says that the letter alone kills.

> *Who also hath made us able ministers of the new testament; not of the letter, but of the spirit: for the letter killeth, but the spirit giveth life. 2 Cor. 3:6*

The New Testament is predominantly comprised of letters written from the apostles to the church. And the Bible says that the letter alone kills, but the spirit gives life. This is not to say that the Scripture is not important in combating the works of the enemy–it is primary.

However, it is to say that the Scripture, without the power of the Holy Spirit breathing on it, will not be effective. And the spirit realm, without the guidance of the Scripture, will only lead us into weirdness and areas of further demonic influence.

"...but mighty through to the pulling down of strongholds. "

What are strongholds? Incorrectly, many are under the presumption or the belief that strongholds are demonic spirits. Strongholds are not demonic spirits. Strongholds are thoughts, contentions, beliefs, traditions, and legalistic rules that the devil sets up in our minds. These things become strongholds, where our mind becomes contrary (enmity) to the mind of God.

Because the carnal mind is enmity against God: for it is not subject to the law of God, neither indeed can be.
Romans 8:7

Another word for strongholds, which comes from the Greek definition of the word is fortresses, and that's what the enemy does. The enemy builds walls in our minds through demonic thoughts–through thoughts that are contrary to the will and Word of God, and the mind of Christ. The enemy sets up fortresses around our mind, and our minds actually become at enmity against the mind of God. And in doing so, the enemy controls our behavior, through the agency of our thoughts.

If we're to ever live victorious lives, if we're to maintain and sustain the deliverance that will come through the Holy Spirit, we must again take on the mind of Christ through the renewing of our mind, through the application of the Word of God.

"...but mighty through God to the pulling down of strongholds."

This lets us know that strongholds are where? Up, not down! Strongholds again are fortresses on our thoughts, fortresses on our minds. And the Word of God, gives us the power to pull those fortresses down, so that we may then be ready to receive and embrace the Word of God. This is specifically why many times it is very difficult to convince people of truth. They have had a way of thinking which has persisted for years. This is why your mind must be constantly, consistently bombarded with the Word of God in every area of your life.

If you're dealing with sickness, and you are of the belief that sometimes God may bring things upon people to teach them something–to teach them righteousness–that thought has to be cast down. The lie has to be pulled down before you can ever embrace the truth about God's will for healing to His people. For the Word of God says "... by [His] stripes ye were healed" (1 Pet. 2:24). Not by His stripes we were stricken and afflicted. By His stripes we were healed.

"Casting down imaginations and every high thing that exhalteth itself against the knowledge of God..."

Here we have the clear indication of ungodly thoughts prevent us from walking in the mind of Christ. It says casting down imaginations. Many times we have thoughts, unholy thoughts, wicked thoughts, or absolutely perverted, evil thoughts. Unknowingly, we may embrace these thoughts as our own, not knowing that these thoughts have been planted by the enemy.

EVIL WICKED IMAGINATIONS

Each and every time you are confronted with evil and wicked imaginations, you must immediately combat them by the Word of God. This simply means that anything contrary to the will of God must be cast down, whether it be ideologies, doctrines, a belief system, traditions, or ways in which we were raised. If those ways are contrary to the Word of God, those thoughts and those beliefs must be cast down. That is the only way we are going to be able to live in the absolute victory that Christ has provided for us.

"...and bringing into captivity every thought to the obedience of Christ."

This again is a work of renewing the mind, which means that every thought—not just some thoughts, or only sexually impure thoughts, but every thought—must be brought in captivity to the obedience of Christ. What is the obedience of Christ? It is His Word. Every thought must become subject to the Word of God.

"...and having in a readiness to revenge all disobedience when disobedience is revealed."

What does this mean? It means that we've failed in the past. We've missed it in the past. The way that we have thought in the past has been incorrect. The way that we have thought in the past has been the way of the world and not the way of God. We're to revenge that disobedience when we begin to walk in obedience to the Word of God.

Meditate on 2 Corinthians 10:3-6. Decide to never let *any* ungodly imagination or thought dwell in your mind.

Renewing the Mind

I beseech you therefore, brethren, by the mercies of God, that ye present your bodies a living sacrifice, holy, acceptable unto God, which is your reasonable service. And be not conformed to this world: but be ye transformed by the renewing of your mind, that ye may prove what is that good, and acceptable, and perfect, will of God. Romans 12:1-2

In Romans 12:1-2, Paul admonishes us that we are to live a holy life, that our lives are to be a living sacrifice for the service of God. Traditionally, when we speak of the issue of holiness, the major concern or emphasis is placed upon issues such as prayer, fasting, and not forsaking the fellowship of yourselves with one another. However, if we dissect the Scripture above, we see that this is achieved by not being conformed to this world. Meaning, being not conformed to this world's thinking, being not conformed to the ways of the world, being not conformed to the ideologies of the world, but being transformed by the renewing of our mind.

The renewing of the mind means that we're to replace our thoughts with the thoughts of God. We're to replace worldly ideologies, concepts and philosophies with the ideologies, concepts and principals of the kingdom of God and the Word of God.

We have traditions in our culture that are contrary to the will and Word of God. Those things are to be replaced by the renewing of our minds through the application of the Word of God, and the appropriation of the Word of God. This is not done by reading the Word of God, nor is it done by just studying the Word of God. This is done by actually reading, studying, confessing and applying the Word of God to the circumstances we encounter daily in our lives.

Renewing the mind is carried out expressly through the profession (rather confession) of the Word.

Let us hold fast the profession of our faith without wavering; (for he is faithful that promised).
Hebrews 10:23

Now you may say I've heard about the concept of renewing the mind. I'm aware that the Bible admonishes us and encourages us to renew our mind. But how does renewing the mind specifically apply to my particular situation and exactly how do I use the Word to renew my mind? It works like this: Let's say that you're having a problem with lust or thoughts that are contrary to the will of God, you must find Scriptures in the Bible that contradict and oppose those thoughts. If you're having impure, unholy thoughts a Scripture that is contrary to those thoughts would be Philip. 4:8:

Finally, brethren, whatsoever things are true, whatsoever things are honest, whatsoever things are just, whatsoever things are pure, whatsoever things are lovely, whatsoever things are of good report; if there be any virtue, and if there be any praise, think on these things.

Another example of this is the issue of fear. If you're dealing with thoughts of fear as we spoke of in charismatic witchcraft, a Scripture to combat that directly would be the spoken, verbal confession of.
2 Timothy 1:7

For God has not given us the spirit of fear, but one of power, of love, and a sound mind. 2 Timothy 1:7 (or as the NIV would say of power, of love, and a disciplined mind.)

When you renew your mind on a continual basis, you actually begin to replace old thoughts with new thoughts.

A transformation in the spirit of your mind begins when you establish a pattern of doing this on a continual basis. There is a renewing of the mind because you actually progress to a point where you no longer have to verbally speak Scriptures to combat those actions and thoughts that are not desirable. It just becomes second nature.

For who hath known the mind of the Lord, that he may instruct him? But we have the mind of Christ.
1 Cor. 2:16

Let this mind be in you, which was also in Christ Jesus.
Philip. 2:5

Renewing the mind is not just a mental ascension of the truth of the Word of God or a memorization of Scripture–though that is most definitely necessary. We're talking about having the mind of Christ, where your thoughts become His thoughts. When you begin to think like Christ, you're no longer being conformed to this world's thinking, but your mind is actually transformed, it's become renewed. You now have the mind of Christ.

You need to realize that the responsibility for renewing your mind is yours. Perhaps you thought your mind was like a VCR, and every time you looked on a man or woman to lust, God was going to do you a favor by inserting a praise and worship video. Wrong! What you choose to think about is a decision you must make–the action is yours. God is so good, all the time, that He's provided you with a sure-fire six-step plan to assist you in controlling your thoughts and renewing your mind in Philippians 4:8. I can not stress enough in this book to meditate on this Scripture.

Finally, brethren, whatsoever things are true, whatsoever things are honest, whatsoever things are just, whatsoever things are pure, whatsoever things are lovely, whatsoever things are of good report; if there be any virtue, and if there be any praise, think on these things. Phillip. 4:8

THE WORD OF THE LORD

And the Lord God says, "I love you and I have confidence in what I've deposited in your spirit. You're coming out of this. It may not be today, it may not be tomorrow, it may not even be next week or next month, but you are coming out. Just keep getting up.

Do you know how many times I'm willing to forgive you? Seventy times seven in one day! Just keep getting up. Because I know that if you really love me, sooner or later you're going to get sick of the mess. Like the prodigal son, one day soon my son or my daughter, you're going to come to your senses. You're going to use the authority I've giving you in My Word to tell the devil where to get off. And when you do, I'll be waiting for you with open arm's.

Yes, I'll be waiting. No condemnation, no long speeches, no rejection, no I told you so, and no, not even punishment. The wages of your sin is punishment enough. The distress that you now experience day in and day out, the estrangement from family and friends is the corruption you reap from your sin. No, my child, all I have waiting for you is love, love, love, love, love. Come back and embrace your place in the kingdom. Come and get back your crown of righteousness. I didn't take it. You just haven't been wearing it.

My child, don't you think it's way past time you stopped acting like what you've become and start acting like who you are. And who are you? You are a King's kid, you are beloved of Me. I've called you with an everlasting love. I've called you to be the first and not the last, the head and not the tail. Be who you are and stop acting like who the lying devil tells you are.

You say, 'But I act like a whore; I'm irresponsible; I'm unfaithful; I'm a fornicator; I'm an adulterer; I'm a failure.' Well, I have one question to ask you. Who told you that? Did I tell you that? Does My Word tell you that? No, My darlings, My sons, it's My goodness that leads you to repentance.

For I say unto you, be healed. I say be delivered, be free. Whom My Son sets free is free indeed. I say receive your healing and go and sin no more . . . Now who says this? Not man, not woman . . . no I say it. Thus says, the LORD. The Lord your God. For I, and I alone am your All and All. The Source of your supply. You need it, I have it . . . For I, and I alone am God, and if I be for you, who can be against you?"

SCRIPTURE REFERENCES

The following compilation of Scriptures, taken from the *Juanita Bynum Topical Bible*, have been included for your reference.

In order to have victory in any area of our lives, we must remain committed to prayer and the study of God's Word. We should know these Scriptures as well as we know our home telephone number or social security number. These Scriptures should become part of your daily arsenal to fight off unholy urges and desires–for the Word of God is the sword of the Spirit.

Finally beloved, remember that God's Word is always there for you–whether you are succeeding or have failed miserably. Renew your mind the Word of God as you decree that henceforth, now and forever more, there will be *No More Sheets!*

Believing in Jesus Christ

Verily, verily, I say unto you, He that believeth on me hath everlasting life. John 6:47

But as many as received him, to them gave he power to become the sons of God, even to them that believe on his name. John 1:12

That whosoever believeth in him should not perish, but have eternal life.   John 3:15

For God so loved the world, that he gave his only begotten Son, that whosoever believeth in him should not perish, but have everlasting life.   John 3:16

For God sent not his Son into the world to condemn the world; but that the world through him might be saved. He that believeth on him is not condemned: but he that believeth not is condemned already, because he hath not believed in the name of the only begotten Son of God.
                                          John 3:17-18

He that believeth on the Son hath everlasting life: and he that believeth not the Son shall not see life; but the wrath of God abideth on him. John 3:36

Verily, verily, I say unto you, He that heareth my word, and believeth on him that sent me, hath everlasting life, and shall not come into condemnation; but is passed from death unto life. John 5:24

I am the bread of life: he that cometh to me shall never hunger; and he that believeth on me shall never thirst.
                                          John 6:32-35

Verily, verily, I say unto you, He that believeth on me hath everlasting life. John 6:47

And we believe and are sure that thou art that Christ, the Son of the living God. John 6:69

I said therefore unto you, that ye shall die in your sins: for if ye believe not that I am he, ye shall die in your sins.
John 8:24

But if I do, though ye believe not me, believe the works: that ye may know, and believe, that the Father is in me, and I in him. John 10:38

But these are written, that ye might believe that Jesus is the Christ, the Son of God; and that believing ye might have life through his name. John 20:31

For he saith, I have heard thee in a time accepted, and in the day of salvation have I succoured thee: behold, now is the accepted time; behold, now is the day of salvation.
2 Corinthians 6:2

THE PLAN OF SALVATION

That if thou shalt confess with thy mouth the Lord Jesus, and shalt believe in thine heart that God hath raised him from the dead, thou shalt be saved. Romans 10:9

For with the heart man believeth unto righteousness; and with the mouth confession is made unto salvation. Romans 10:10

HOW TO BE SAVED

ADMIT THAT YOU HAVE SINNED, CONFESS TO GOD, AND REPENT.

Confess—speak aloud—that Jesus Christ is Lord, the Son of God.

Believe in your heart—inner most being, spirit, the real you—that God raised Jesus Christ from the dead.

After completing the above three steps, according to the Word of God, you are now saved and have eternal life through Jesus Christ.

How Do You Know You Are Really Saved

For whosoever shall call upon the name of the Lord shall be saved. Romans 10:1

Verily, verily, I say unto you, He that heareth my word, and believeth on him that sent me, hath everlasting life, and shall not come into condemnation; but is passed from death unto life. John 5:24

And I give unto them eternal life; and they shall never perish, neither shall any man pluck them out of my hand.
John 10:28

These things have I written unto you that believe on the name of the Son of God; that ye may know that ye have eternal life, and that ye may believe on the name of the Son of God. 1 John 5:13

For with the heart man believeth unto righteousness; and with the mouth confession is made unto salvation.
Romans 10:10

Saved by Grace

Even when we were dead in sins, hath quickened us together with Christ, by grace ye are saved. Ephesians 2:5

For by grace are ye saved through faith; and that not of your-selves: it is the gift of God. Ephesians 2:8

For the grace of God that bringeth salvation hath appeared to all men. Titus 2:11

Who hath saved us, and called us with an holy calling, not according to our works, but according to his own purpose and grace, which was given us in Christ Jesus before the world began. 2 Timothy 1:9

CONTROLLING LUST

Lust not after her beauty in thine heart; neither let her take thee with her eyelids. Proverbs 6:25

But I say unto you, That whosoever looketh on a woman to lust after her hath committed adultery with her already in his heart. Matthew 5:28

And the cares of this world, and the deceitfulness of riches, and the lusts of other things entering in, choke the word, and it becometh unfruitful. Mark 4:19

Wherefore God also gave them up to uncleanness through the lusts of their own hearts, to dishonour their own bodies between themselves. Romans 1:24

Let not sin therefore reign in your mortal body, that ye should obey it in the lusts thereof. Romans 6:12

But put ye on the Lord Jesus Christ, and make not provision for the flesh, to fulfil the lusts thereof. Romans 13:14

Now these things were our examples, to the intent we should not lust after evil things, as they also lusted.

1 Corinthians 10:6

This I say then, Walk in the Spirit, and ye shall not fulfill the lust of the flesh. For the flesh lusteth against the Spirit, and the Spirit against the flesh: and these are contrary the one to the other: so that ye cannot do the things that ye would. Galatians 5:16-17

And they that are Christ's have crucified the flesh with the affections and lusts. Galatians 5:24

Wherein in time past ye walked according to the course of this world, according to the prince of the power of the air, the spirit that now worketh in the children of disobedience: Among whom also we all had our conversation in times past in the lusts of our flesh, fulfilling the desires of the flesh and of the mind; and were by nature the children of wrath, even as others. But God, who is rich in mercy, for his great love wherewith he loved us, Even when we were dead in sins, hath quickened us together with Christ, (by grace ye are saved;) And hath raised us up together, and made us sit together in heavenly places in Christ Jesus. Ephesians 2:2-6

Flee also youthful lusts: but follow righteousness, faith, charity, peace, with them that call on the Lord out of a pure heart. 2 Timothy 2:22

Teaching us that, denying ungodliness and worldly lusts, we should live soberly, righteously, and godly, in this present world. Titus 2:12

Let no man say when he is tempted, I am tempted of God: for God cannot be tempted with evil, neither tempteth he any man: But every man is tempted, when he is drawn away of his own lust, and enticed. Then when lust hath conceived, it bringeth forth sin: and sin, when it is finished, bringeth forth death. James 1:13-15

As obedient children, not fashioning yourselves according to the former lusts in your ignorance. 1 Peter 1:14

Dearly beloved, I beseech you as strangers and pilgrims, abstain from fleshly lusts, which war against the soul.

1 Peter 2:11

That he no longer should live the rest of his time in the flesh to the lusts of men, but to the will of God. 1 Peter 4:2

Whereby are given unto us exceeding great and precious promises: that by these ye might be partakers of the divine nature, having escaped the corruption that is in the world through lust. 2 Peter 1:4

For all that is in the world, the lust of the flesh, and the lust of the eyes, and the pride of life, is not of the Father, but is of the world. And the world passeth away, and the lust thereof: but he that doeth the will of God abideth for ever.

1 John 2:16-17

THE TEMPLE OF THE HOLY SPIRIT

Know ye not that ye are the temple of God, and that the Spirit of God dwelleth in you? If any man defile the temple of God, him shall God destroy; for the temple of God is holy, which temple ye are. 1 Corinthians 3:16-17

What? know ye not that your body is the temple of the Holy Ghost which is in you, which ye have of God, and ye are not your own? For ye are bought with a price: therefore glorify God in your body, and in your spirit, which are God's.

1 Corinthians 6:19-20

Whether therefore ye eat, or drink, or whatsoever ye do, do all to the glory of God. 1 Corinthians 10:31

SEX BEFORE MARRIAGE

But that we write unto them, that they abstain from pollutions of idols, and from fornication, and from things strangled, and from blood. Acts 15:20

That ye abstain from meats offered to idols, and from blood, and from things strangled, and from fornication: from which if ye keep yourselves, ye shall do well. Fare ye well.
Acts 15:29

Know ye not that your bodies are the members of Christ? shall I then take the members of Christ, and make them the members of an harlot? God forbid. What? know ye not that he which is joined to an harlot is one body? for two, saith he, shall be one flesh. 1 Corinthians 6:15-16

Flee fornication. Every sin that a man doeth is without the body; but he that commiteth fornication sinneth against his own body. What? know ye not that your body is the temple of the Holy Ghost which is in you, which ye have of God, and ye are not your own? For ye are bought with a price: therefore glorify God in your body, and in your spirit, which are God's. 1 Corinthians 6:18-20

Now concerning the things whereof ye wrote unto me: It is good for a man not to touch a woman. Nevertheless, to avoid fornication, let every man have his own wife, and let every woman have her own husband. 1 Corinthians 7:1-2

Neither let us commit fornication, as some of them committed, and fell in one day three and twenty thousand.
1 Corinthians 10:8

But fornication, and all uncleanness, or covetousness, let it not be once named among you, as becometh saints.

Ephesians 5:3

For this is the will of God, even your sanctification, that ye should abstain from fornication: 1 Thessalonians 4:3

SEX IS ONLY FOR MARRIED COUPLES

Let the husband render unto the wife due benevolence: and likewise also the wife unto the husband. The wife hath not power of her own body, but the husband: and likewise also the husband hath not power of his own body, but the wife. Defraud ye not one the other, except it be with consent for a time, that ye may give yourselves to fasting and prayer; and come together again, that Satan tempt you not for your incontinency. 1 Corinthians 7:3-5

THE CONSEQUENCES OF FORNICATION

Now the works of the flesh are manifest, which are these; Adultery, fornication, uncleanness, lasciviousness, Envyings, murders, drunkenness, revellings, and such like: of the which I tell you before, as I have also told you in time past, that they which do such things shall not inherit the kingdom of God. Galatians 5:19,21

Marriage is honourable in all, and the bed undefiled: but whoremongers and adulterers God will judge. Hebrews 13:4

Even as Sodom and Gomorrha, and the cities about them in like manner, giving themselves over to fornication, and going after strange flesh, are set forth for an example, suffering the vengeance of eternal fire. Jude 1:7

Adultery

Thou shalt not commit adultery. Exodus 20:14

And the man that committeth adultery with another man's wife, even he that committeth adultery with his neighbour's wife, the adulterer and the adulteress shall surely be put to death. Leviticus 20:10

Neither shalt thou commit adultery. Deuteronomy 5:18

Such is the way of an adulterous woman; she eateth, and wipeth her mouth, and saith, I have done no wickedness.
Proverbs 30:20

But I say unto you, That whosoever looketh on a woman to lust after her hath committed adultery with her already in his heart. Matthew 5:28

For by means of a whorish woman a man is brought to a piece of bread: and the adulteress will hunt for the precious life. Proverbs 6:26

But whoso committeth adultery with a woman lacketh understanding: he that doeth it destroyeth his own soul.
Proverbs 6:32

Know ye not that the unrighteous shall not inherit the kingdom of God? Be not deceived: neither fornicators, nor idolaters, nor adulterers, nor effeminate, nor abusers of themselves with mankind. 1 Corinthians 6:9

Homosexuality and Lesbianism

Thou shalt not lie with mankind, as with womankind: it is abomination. Leviticus 18:22

If a man also lie with mankind, as he lieth with a woman, both of them have committed an abomination: they shall surely be put to death; their blood shall be upon them.

Leviticus 20:13

Wherefore God also gave them up to uncleanness through the lusts of their own hearts, to dishonour their own bodies between themselves. Romans 1:24

For this cause God gave them up unto vile affections: for even their women did change the natural use into that which is against nature: And likewise also the men, leaving the natural use of the woman, burned in their lust one toward another; men with men working that which is unseemly, and receiving in themselves that recompence of their error which was meet. And even as they did not like to retain God in their knowledge, God gave them over to a reprobate mind, to do those things which are not convenient.

Romans 1:26-28

Without understanding, covenantbreakers, without natural affection, implacable, unmerciful. Romans 1:31

Mortify therefore your members which are upon the earth; fornication, uncleanness, inordinate affection, evil concupiscence, and covetousness, which is idolatry.

Colossians 3:5

Without natural affection, trucebreakers, false accusers, incontinent, fierce, despisers of those that are good.

2 Timothy 3:3

OVERCOMING SIN

All unrighteousness is sin: and there is a sin not unto death.

1 John 5:17

Jesus answered them, Verily, verily, I say unto you, Whosoever committeth sin is the servant of sin. John 8:34

These six things doth the Lord hate: yea, seven are an abomination unto him. A proud look, a lying tongue, and hands that shed innocent blood. An heart that deviseth wicked imaginations, feet that be swift in running to mischief, A false witness that speaketh lies, and he that soweth discord among brethren. Proverbs 6:16-19

Now the works of the flesh are manifest, which are these; Adultery, fornication, uncleanness, lasciviousness, Idolatry, witchcraft, hatred, variance, emulations, wrath, strife, seditions, heresies, envyings, murders, drunkenness, revellings, and such like: of the which I tell you before, as I have also told you in time past, that they which do such things shall not inherit the kingdom of God. Galatians 5:19-21

He that committeth sin is of the devil; for the devil sinneth from the beginning. For this purpose the Son of God was manifested, that he might destroy the works of the devil. Whosoever is born of God doth not commit sin; for his seed remaineth in him: and he cannot sin, because he is born of God. In this the children of God are manifest, and the children of the devil: whosoever doeth not righteousness is not of God, neither he that loveth not his brother.

1 John 3:8-10

Whosoever abideth in him sinneth not: whosoever sinneth hath not seen him, neither known him. 1 John 3:6

Whosoever is born of God doth not commit sin; for his seed remaineth in him: and he cannot sin, because he is born of God. 1 John 3:9

We know that whosoever is born of God sinneth not; but he that is begotten of God keepeth himself, and that wicked one toucheth him not. 1 John 5:18

There is a way that seemeth right unto a man, but the end thereof are the ways of death. Proverbs 16:25

And he that doubteth is damned if he eat, because he eateth not of faith: for whatsoever is not of faith is sin.
Romans 14:23

But the man who has doubts—misgivings, an uneasy conscience-about eating, and then eats [perhaps because of you], stands condemned [before God], because he is not true to his convictions and he does not act from faith. For whatever does not originate and proceed from faith is sin—that is, whatever is done without a conviction of its approval by God is sinful. Romans 14:23 AMP

SECRET SINS

But if ye will not do so, behold, ye have sinned against the Lord: and be sure your sin will find you out.
Numbers 32:23

He that covereth his sins shall not prosper: but whoso confesseth and forsaketh them shall have mercy.
Proverbs 28:13

For God shall bring every work into judgment, with every secret thing, whether it be good, or whether it be evil.
Ecclesiastes 12:14

For there is nothing covered, that shall not be revealed; neither hid, that shall not be known. Therefore whatsoever ye have spoken in darkness shall be heard in the light; and that which ye have spoken in the ear in closets shall be proclaimed upon the housetops. Luke 12:2-3

In the day when God shall judge the secrets of men by Jesus Christ according to my gospel. Romans 2:16

Sowing Sin and Reaping the Consequences of Sin

But he that doeth wrong shall receive for the wrong which he hath done: and there is no respect of persons.
                                        Colossians 3:25

Even as I have seen, they that plow iniquity, and sow wickedness, reap the same. Job 4:8

Evil pursueth sinners: but to the righteous good shall be repayed. Proverbs 13:21

Whoso rewardeth evil for good, evil shall not depart from his house. Proverbs 17:13

He that soweth iniquity shall reap vanity: and the rod of his anger shall fail. Proverbs 22:8

Whoso causeth the righteous to go astray in an evil way, he shall fall himself into his own pit: but the upright shall have good things in possession. Proverbs 28:10

Ye have plowed wickedness, ye have reaped iniquity; ye have eaten the fruit of lies: because thou didst trust in thy way, in the multitude of thy mighty men. Hosea 10:13

For the wages of sin is death; but the gift of God is eternal life through Jesus Christ our Lord. Romans 6:23

Be not deceived; God is not mocked: for whatsoever a man soweth, that shall he also reap. For he that soweth to his flesh shall of the flesh reap corruption; but he that soweth to the Spirit shall of the Spirit reap life everlasting.

Galatians 6:7-8

SIN GIVES SATAN ENTRANCE INTO YOUR LIFE

Be ye angry, and sin not: let not the sun go down upon your wrath: Neither give place to the devil. Ephesians 4:26-27

Afterward Jesus findeth him in the temple, and said unto him, Behold, thou art made whole: sin no more, lest a worse thing come unto thee. John 5:14

To whom ye forgive any thing, I forgive also: for if I forgave any thing, to whom I forgave it, for your sakes forgave I it in the person of Christ; Lest satan should get an advantage of us: for we are not ignorant of his devices.

2 Corinthians 2:10-11

Not a novice, lest being lifted up with pride he fall into the condemnation of the devil. Moreover he must have a good report of them which are without; lest he fall into reproach and the snare of the devil. 1 Timothy 3:6-7

Then came Peter to him, and said, Lord, how oft shall my brother sin against me, and I forgive him? till seven times? Jesus saith unto him, I say not unto thee, Until seven times: but, Until seventy times seven. Therefore is the kingdom of heaven likened unto a certain king, which would take account of his servants. Then his lord, after that he had called him, said unto him, O thou wicked servant, I forgave thee all that debt, because thou desiredst me: Shouldest not thou also have had compassion on thy fellowservant, even as I had pity on thee? And his lord was wroth, and delivered him to the tormentors, till he should pay all that was due unto him. So likewise shall my heavenly Father do also unto you, if ye from your hearts forgive not every one his brother their trespasses. Matthew 18:21-23,32-35

Repentance

DEFINITION: Repent means to change one's mind or purpose with regard to sin, a sorrow for sin

Or despisest thou the riches of his goodness and forbearance and longsuffering; not knowing that the goodness of God leadeth thee to repentance? Romans 2:4

The Lord is not slack concerning his promise, as some men count slackness; but is longsuffering to us-ward, not willing that any should perish, but that all should come to repentance. 2 Peter 3:9

I tell you, Nay: but, except ye repent, ye shall all likewise perish. Luke 13:3

Therefore I will judge you, O house of Israel, every one according to his ways, saith the Lord God. Repent, and turn yourselves from all your transgressions; so iniquity shall not be your ruin. Ezekiel 18:30

For godly sorrow worketh repentance to salvation not to be repented of: but the sorrow of the world worketh death.
2 Corinthians 7:10

Say unto them, As I live, saith the Lord God, I have no pleasure in the death of the wicked; but that the wicked turn from his way and live: turn ye, turn ye from your evil ways; for why will ye die, O house of Israel? Ezekiel 33:11

And saying, The time is fulfilled, and the kingdom of God is at hand: repent ye, and believe the gospel. Mark 1:15

Repent ye therefore, and be converted, that your sins may be blotted out, when the times of refreshing shall come from the presence of the Lord. Acts 3:19

From that time Jesus began to preach, and to say, Repent: for the kingdom of heaven is at hand. Matthew 4:17

I say unto you, that likewise joy shall be in heaven over one sinner that repenteth, more than over ninety and nine just persons, which need no repentance. Luke 15:7

When Jesus heard it, he saith unto them, They that are whole have no need of the physician, but they that are sick: I came not to call the righteous, but sinners to repentance.

Mark 2:17

And the times of this ignorance God winked at; but now commandeth all men every where to repent. Acts 17:30

Likewise, I say unto you, there is joy in the presence of the angels of God over one sinner that repenteth. Luke 15:10

Him hath God exalted with his right hand to be a Prince and a Saviour, for to give repentance to Israel, and forgiveness of sins. Acts 5:31

PROOF OF REPENTANCE

I thought on my ways, and turned my feet unto thy testimonies. Psalms 119:59

But shewed first unto them of Damascus, and at Jerusalem, and throughout all the coasts of Judaea, and then to the

NO MORE SHEETS DEVOTIONAL

Gentiles, that they should repent and turn to God, and do works meet for repentance. Acts 26:20

Bring forth therefore fruits meet for repentance.

Matthew 3:8

CONFESS THE SIN

He that covereth his sins shall not prosper: but whoso confesseth and forsaketh them shall have mercy.

Proverbs 28:13

And it shall be, when he shall be guilty in one of these things, that he shall confess that he hath sinned in that thing.

Leviticus 5:5

If we confess our sins, he is faithful and just to forgive us our sins, and to cleanse us from all unrighteousness. 1 John 1:9

And the seed of Israel separated themselves from all strangers, and stood and confessed their sins, and the iniquities of their fathers. Nehemiah 9:2

I acknowledged my sin unto thee, and mine iniquity have I not hid. I said, I will confess my transgressions unto the Lord; and thou forgavest the iniquity of my sin. Selah. Psalms 32:5

And were baptized of him in Jordan, confessing their sins.

Matthew 3:6

And many that believed came, and confessed, and shewed their deeds. Acts 19:18

Confess your faults one to another, and pray one for another, that ye may be healed. The effectual fervent prayer of a righteous man availeth much. James 5:16

DELIVERANCE FROM SIN

And she shall bring forth a son, and thou shalt call his name Jesus: for he shall save his people from their sins.

Matthew 1:21

The next day John seeth Jesus coming unto him, and saith, Behold the Lamb of God, which taketh away the sin of the world. John 1:29

For he hath made him to be sin for us, who knew no sin; that we might be made the righteousness of God in him.

2 Corinthians 5:21

For when we were yet without strength, in due time Christ died for the ungodly. Romans 5:6

But God commendeth his love toward us, in that, while we were yet sinners, Christ died for us. Romans 5:8

For the law of the Spirit of life in Christ Jesus hath made me free from the law of sin and death. Romans 8:2

To wit, that God was in Christ, reconciling the world unto himself, not imputing their trespasses unto them; and hath committed unto us the word of reconciliation.

2 Corinthians 5:19

Who gave himself for our sins, that he might deliver us from this present evil world, according to the will of God and our Father. Galatians 1:4

And, having made peace through the blood of his cross, by him to reconcile all things unto himself; by him, I say, whether they be things in earth, or things in heaven.

Colossians 1:20

SINS CLEANSED BY THE BLOOD OF JESUS

But now in Christ Jesus ye who sometimes were far off are made nigh by the blood of Christ. Ephesians 2:13

In whom we have redemption through his blood, even the forgiveness of sins. Colossians 1:14

For this is my blood of the new testament, which is shed for many for the remission of sins. Matthew 26:28

And from Jesus Christ, who is the faithful witness, and the first begotten of the dead, and the prince of the kings of the earth. Unto him that loved us, and washed us from our sins in his own blood. Revelation 1:5

GOD WILL FORGIVE YOUR SINS

For if ye turn again unto the Lord, your brethren and your children shall find compassion before them that lead them captive, so that they shall come again into this land: for the Lord your God is gracious and merciful, and will not turn away his face from you, if ye return unto him.

2 Chronicles 30:9

Blessed is he whose transgression is forgiven, whose sin is covered. Blessed is the man unto whom the Lord imputeth not iniquity, and in whose spirit there is no guile.

Psalms 32:1-2

I acknowledged my sin unto thee, and mine iniquity have I not hid. I said, I will confess my transgressions unto the Lord; and thou forgavest the iniquity of my sin. Selah. Psalms 32:5

For thou, Lord, art good, and ready to forgive; and plenteous in mercy unto all them that call upon thee. Psalms 86:5

And the inhabitant shall not say, I am sick: the people that dwell therein shall be forgiven their iniquity. Isaiah 33:24

I have blotted out, as a thick cloud, thy transgressions, and, as a cloud, thy sins: return unto me; for I have redeemed thee. Isaiah 44:22

Who is a God like unto thee, that pardoneth iniquity, and passeth by the transgression of the remnant of his heritage? he retaineth not his anger for ever, because he delighteth in mercy. He will turn again, he will have compassion upon us; he will subdue our iniquities; and thou wilt cast all their sins into the depths of the sea. Micah 7:18-19

And forgive us our debts, as we forgive our debtors.
Matthew 6:12

For if ye forgive men their trespasses, your heavenly Father will also forgive you: But if ye forgive not men their trespasses, neither will your Father forgive your trespasses.
Matthew 6:14-15

In whom we have redemption through his blood, the forgiveness of sins, according to the riches of his grace.
Ephesians 1:7

For I will be merciful to their unrighteousness, and their sins and their iniquities will I remember no more. Hebrews 8:12

But this man, after he had offered one sacrifice for sins for ever, sat down on the right hand of God. Hebrews 10:12

And their sins and iniquities will I remember no more. Now where remission of these is, there is no more offering for sin.
Hebrews 10:17-18

If we confess our sins, he is faithful and just to forgive us our sins, and to cleanse us from all unrighteousness. 1 John 1:9

My little children, these things write I unto you, that ye sin not. And if any man sin, we have an advocate with the Father, Jesus Christ the righteous: And he is the propitiation for our sins: and not for ours only, but also for the sins of the whole world. 1 John 2:1-2

God Will Not Remember Your Sins

And they shall teach no more every man his neighbour, and every man his brother, saying, Know the Lord: for they shall all know me, from the least of them unto the greatest of them, saith the Lord; for I will forgive their iniquity, and I will remember their sin no more. Jeremiah 31:34

He will turn again, he will have compassion upon us; he will subdue our iniquities; and thou wilt cast all their sins into the depths of the sea. Micah 7:19

This is the covenant that I will make with them after those days, saith the Lord, I will put my laws into their hearts, and in their minds will I write them; And their sins and iniquities will I remember no more. Hebrews 10:16-17

God Will Blot Out Your Sins

I, even I, am he that blotteth out thy transgressions for mine own sake, and will not remember thy sins. Isaiah 43:25

I have blotted out, as a thick cloud, thy transgressions, and, as a cloud, thy sins: return unto me; for I have redeemed thee. Isaiah 44:22

Repent ye therefore, and be converted, that your sins may be blotted out, when the times of refreshing shall come from the presence of the Lord. Acts 3:19

OVERCOMING GUILT

Brethren, I count not myself to have apprehended: but this one thing I do, forgetting those things which are behind, and reaching forth unto those things which are before.

Philippians 3:13

For if ye turn again unto the Lord, your brethren and your children shall find compassion before them that lead them captive, so that they shall come again into this land: for the Lord your God is gracious and merciful, and will not turn away his face from you, if ye return unto him.

2 Chronicles 30:9

As far as the east is from the west, so far hath he removed our transgressions from us. Psalms 103:12

Let the wicked forsake his way, and the unrighteous man his thoughts: and let him return unto the Lord, and he will have mercy upon him; and to our God, for he will abundantly pardon. Isaiah 55:7

And I will cleanse them from all their iniquity, whereby they have sinned against me; and I will pardon all their iniquities, whereby they have sinned, and whereby they have transgressed against me. Jeremiah 33:8

For God sent not his Son into the world to condemn the world; but that the world through him might be saved. He that believeth on him is not condemned: but he that believeth not is condemned already, because he hath not believed in the name of the only begotten Son of God.

John 3:17-18

Therefore if any man be in Christ, he is a new creature: old things are passed away; behold, all things are become new.

2 Corinthians 5:17

For I will be merciful to their unrighteousness, and their sins and their iniquities will I remember no more. Hebrews 8:12

Let us draw near with a true heart in full assurance of faith, having our hearts sprinkled from an evil conscience, and our bodies washed with pure water. Hebrews 10:22

But if we walk in the light, as he is in the light, we have fellowship one with another, and the blood of Jesus Christ his Son cleanseth us from all sin. 1 John 1:7

If we confess our sins, he is faithful and just to forgive us our sins, and to cleanse us from all unrighteousness. 1 John 1:9

I write unto you, little children, because your sins are forgiven you for his name's sake. 1 John 2:12

Overcoming Condemnation

For God sent not his Son into the world to condemn the world; but that the world through him might be saved.

John 3:17

Verily, verily, I say unto you, He that heareth my word, and believeth on him that sent me, hath everlasting life, and shall not come into condemnation; but is passed from death unto life. John 5:24

There is therefore now no condemnation to them which are in Christ Jesus, who walk not after the flesh, but after the Spirit. Romans 8:1

For if our heart condemn us, God is greater than our heart, and knoweth all things. Beloved, if our heart condemn us not, then have we confidence toward God. 1 John 3:20-21

BACKSLIDER

DEFINITION: A CHRISTIAN THAT NO LONGER WALKS IN FELLOWSHIP WITH GOD NOR OBEYS HIS WORD

As a dog returneth to his vomit, so a fool returneth to his folly. Proverbs 26:11

The backslider in heart shall be filled with his own ways: and a good man shall be satisfied from himself. Proverbs 14:14

Thine own wickedness shall correct thee, and thy backslidings shall reprove thee: know therefore and see that it is an evil thing and bitter, that thou hast forsaken the Lord thy God, and that my fear is not in thee, saith the Lord God of hosts. Jeremiah 2:19

Go and proclaim these words toward the north, and say, Return, thou backsliding Israel, saith the Lord; and I will not cause mine anger to fall upon you: for I am merciful, saith the Lord, and I will not keep anger for ever.
Jeremiah 3:12

Turn, O backsliding children, saith the Lord; for I am married unto you: and I will take you one of a city, and two of a family, and I will bring you to Zion. Jeremiah 3:14

Return, ye backsliding children, and I will heal your backslidings. Behold, we come unto thee; for thou art the Lord our God. Jeremiah 3:22

O Israel, return unto the Lord thy God; for thou hast fallen by thine iniquity. Hosea 14:1

But now, after that ye have known God, or rather are known of God, how turn ye again to the weak and beggarly elements, whereunto ye desire again to be in bondage?

Galatians 4:9

Having damnation, because they have cast off their first faith.

1 Timothy 5:12

AVOIDING OR BREAKING BAD RELATIONSHIPS

Blessed is the man that walketh not in the counsel of the ungodly, nor standeth in the way of sinners, nor sitteth in the seat of the scornful. Psalms 1:1

Depart from me, ye evildoers: for I will keep the commandments of my God. Psalms 119:115

Forsake the foolish, and live; and go in the way of understanding. Proverbs 9:6

The thoughts of the righteous are right: but the counsels of the wicked are deceit. Proverbs 12:5

He that tilleth his land shall be satisfied with bread: but he that followeth vain persons is void of understanding.

Proverbs 12:11

He that walketh with wise men shall be wise: but a companion of fools shall be destroyed. Proverbs 13:20

Go from the presence of a foolish man, when thou perceivest not in him the lips of knowledge. Proverbs 14:7

Better it is to be of an humble spirit with the lowly, than to divide the spoil with the proud. Proverbs 16:19

A violent man enticeth his neighbour, and leadeth him into the way that is not good. Proverbs 16:29

The man that wandereth out of the way of understanding shall remain in the congregation of the dead. Proverbs 21:16

Make no friendship with an angry man; and with a furious man thou shalt not go. Lest thou learn his ways, and get a snare to thy soul. Proverbs 22:24-25

Be not thou envious against evil men, neither desire to be with them. Proverbs 24:1

Whoso keepeth the law is a wise son: but he that is a companion of riotous men shameth his father. Proverbs 28:7

Whoso loveth wisdom rejoiceth his father: but he that keepeth company with harlots spendeth his substance.
Proverbs 29:3

I sat not in the assembly of the mockers, nor rejoiced; I sat alone because of thy hand: for thou hast filled me with indignation. Jeremiah 15:17

Blessed are ye, when men shall hate you, and when they shall separate you from their company, and shall reproach you, and cast out your name as evil, for the Son of man's sake. Luke 6:22

I wrote unto you in an epistle not to company with fornicators: Yet not altogether with the fornicators of this world, or

NO MORE SHEETS DEVOTIONAL

with the covetous, or extortioners, or with idolaters; for then must ye needs go out of the world. But now I have written unto you not to keep company, if any man that is called a brother be a fornicator, or covetous, or an idolater, or a railer, or a drunkard, or an extortioner; with such an one no not to eat. 1 Corinthians 5:9-11

Ye cannot drink the cup of the Lord, and the cup of devils: ye cannot be partakers of the Lord's table, and of the table of devils. 1 Corinthians 10:21

Be not deceived: evil communications corrupt good manners. 1 Corinthians 15:33

Be ye not unequally yoked together with unbelievers: for what fellowship hath righteousness with unrighteousness? and what communion hath light with darkness? And what concord hath Christ with Belial? or what part hath he that believeth with an infidel? 2 Corinthians 6:14-15

And what agreement hath the temple of God with idols? for ye are the temple of the living God; as God hath said, I will dwell in them, and walk in them; and I will be their God, and they shall be my people. Wherefore come out from among them, and be ye separate, saith the Lord, and touch not the unclean thing; and I will receive you, And will be a Father unto you, and ye shall be my sons and daughters, saith the Lord Almighty. 2 Corinthians 6:16-18

And have no fellowship with the unfruitful works of darkness, but rather reprove them. Ephesians 5:11

Abstain from all appearance of evil. 1 Thessalonians 5:22

If ye then be risen with Christ, seek those things which are above, where Christ sitteth on the right hand of God.

Colossians 3:1

Ye adulterers and adulteresses, know ye not that the friendship of the world is enmity with God? whosoever therefore will be a friend of the world is the enemy of God. James 4:4

LONELINESS

And, behold, I am with thee, and will keep thee in all places whither thou goest, and will bring thee again into this land; for I will not leave thee, until I have done that which I have spoken to thee of. Genesis 28:15

Be strong and of a good courage, fear not, nor be afraid of them: for the Lord thy God, he it is that doth go with thee; he will not fail thee, nor forsake thee. Deuteronomy 31:6

The Lord also will be a refuge for the oppressed, a refuge in times of trouble. And they that know thy name will put their trust in thee: for thou, Lord, hast not forsaken them that seek thee. Psalms 9:9-10

For the people shall dwell in Zion at Jerusalem: thou shalt weep no more: he will be very gracious unto thee at the voice of thy cry; when he shall hear it, he will answer thee.

Isaiah 30:19

Fear thou not; for I am with thee: be not dismayed; for I am thy God: I will strengthen thee; yea, I will help thee; yea, I will uphold thee with the right hand of my righteousness.

Isaiah 41:10

In all their affliction he was afflicted, and the angel of his presence saved them: in his love and in his pity he redeemed them; and he bare them, and carried them all the days of old. Isaiah 63:9

Am I a God at hand, saith the Lord, and not a God afar off?
Jeremiah 23:23

Teaching them to observe all things whatsoever I have commanded you: and, lo, I am with you alway, even unto the end of the world. Amen. Matthew 28:20

I will not leave you comfortless: I will come to you.
John 14:18

Who shall separate us from the love of Christ? shall tribulation, or distress, or persecution, or famine, or nakedness, or peril, or sword? As it is written, For thy sake we are killed all the day long; we are accounted as sheep for the slaughter. Nay, in all these things we are more than conquerors through him that loved us. For I am persuaded, that neither death, nor life, nor angels, nor principalities, nor powers, nor things present, nor things to come, Nor height, nor depth, nor any other creature, shall be able to separate us from the love of God, which is in Christ Jesus our Lord. Romans 8:35-39

Casting all your care upon him; for he careth for you.
1 Peter 5:7

Ye are of God, little children, and have overcome them: because greater is he that is in you, than he that is in the world. 1 John 4:4

PRAYER

Let us therefore come boldly unto the throne of grace, that we may obtain mercy, and find grace to help in time of need.

Hebrews 4:16

Ask, and it shall be given you; seek, and ye shall find; knock, and it shall be opened unto you: For every one that asketh receiveth; and he that seeketh findeth; and to him that knocketh it shall be opened. Or what man is there of you, whom if his son ask bread, will he give him a stone? Or if he ask a fish, will he give him a serpent? If ye then, being evil, know how to give good gifts unto your children, how much more shall your Father which is in heaven give good things to them that ask him? Matthew 7:7-11

PRAYING IN THE NAME OF JESUS

Again I say unto you, That if two of you shall agree on earth as touching any thing that they shall ask, it shall be done for them of my Father which is in heaven. For where two or three are gathered together in my name, there am I in the midst of them. Matthew 18:19-20

And whatsoever ye shall ask in my name, that will I do, that the Father may be glorified in the Son. If ye shall ask any thing in my name, I will do it. John 14:13-14

Ye have not chosen me, but I have chosen you, and ordained you, that ye should go and bring forth fruit, and that your fruit should remain: that whatsoever ye shall ask of the Father in my name, he may give it you. John 15:16

And in that day ye shall ask me nothing. Verily, verily, I say unto you, Whatsoever ye shall ask the Father in my name, he will give it you. Hitherto have ye asked nothing in my name: ask, and ye shall receive, that your joy may be full.

John 16:23-24

At that day ye shall ask in my name: and I say not unto you, that I will pray the Father for you. John 16:26

God Hears Your Prayers

Am I a God at hand, saith the Lord, and not a God afar off?

Jeremiah 23:23

But know that the Lord hath set apart him that is godly for himself: the Lord will hear when I call unto him. Psalms 4:3

My voice shalt thou hear in the morning, O Lord; in the morning will I direct my prayer unto thee, and will look up.

Psalms 5:3

I waited patiently for the Lord; and he inclined unto me, and heard my cry. Psalms 40:1

Evening, and morning, and at noon, will I pray, and cry aloud: and he shall hear my voice. Psalms 55:17

The Lord is far from the wicked: but he heareth the prayer of the righteous. Proverbs 15:29

The eyes of the Lord are upon the righteous, and his ears are open unto their cry. Psalms 34:15

Therefore I will look unto the Lord; I will wait for the God of my salvation: my God will hear me. Micah 7:7

And this is the confidence that we have in him, that, if we ask any thing according to his will, he heareth us: And if we know that he hear us, whatsoever we ask, we know that we have the petitions that we desired of him. 1 John 5:14-15

PRAYING IN FAITH

Jesus answered and said unto them, Verily I say unto you, If ye have faith, and doubt not, ye shall not only do this which is done to the fig tree, but also if ye shall say unto this mountain, Be thou removed, and be thou cast into the sea; it shall be done. And all things, whatsoever ye shall ask in prayer, believing, ye shall receive. Matthew 21:21-22

Jesus said unto him, If thou canst believe, all things are possible to him that believeth. And straightway the father of the child cried out, and said with tears, Lord, I believe; help thou mine unbelief. Mark 9:23-24

Therefore I say unto you, What things soever ye desire, when ye pray, believe that ye receive them, and ye shall have them.
Mark 11:24

MEDITATING ON GOD'S WORD

DEFINITIONS FOR MEDITATING
1. TO CARE FOR, TO ATTEND TO, PRACTICE, TO PONDER, OR IMAGINE
2. TO PASS SOME TIME THINKING IN A QUIET WAY; REFLECT
3. TO PLAN OR CONSIDER

This book of the law shall not depart out of thy mouth; but thou shalt meditate therein day and night, that thou mayest observe to do according to all that is written therein: for then thou shalt make thy way prosperous, and then thou shalt have good success. Joshua 1:8

But his delight is in the law of the Lord; and in his law doth he meditate day and night. Psalms 1:2

Let the words of my mouth, and the meditation of my heart, be acceptable in thy sight, O Lord, my strength, and my redeemer. Psalms 19:14

My mouth shall speak of wisdom; and the meditation of my heart shall be of understanding. Psalms 49:3

When I remember thee upon my bed, and meditate on thee in the night watches. Psalms 63:6

I will meditate also of all thy work, and talk of thy doings.
Psalms 77:12

I will meditate in thy precepts, and have respect unto thy ways. Psalms 119:15

Princes also did sit and speak against me: but thy servant did meditate in thy statutes. Psalms 119:23

My hands also will I lift up unto thy commandments, which I have loved; and I will meditate in thy statutes.
Psalms 119:48

O how love I thy law! it is my meditation all the day.
Psalms 119:97

I have more understanding than all my teachers: for thy testimonies are my meditation. Psalms 119:99

Mine eyes prevent the night watches, that I might meditate in thy word. Psalms 119:148

I remember the days of old; I meditate on all thy works; I muse on the work of thy hands. Psalms 143:5

Till I come, give attendance to reading, to exhortation, to doctrine. Meditate upon these things; give thyself wholly to them; that thy profiting may appear to all. 1 Timothy 4:13,15

THE CLEANSING OF THE WORD OF GOD

Wherewithal shall a young man cleanse his way? by taking heed thereto according to thy word. Psalms 119:9

Seeing ye have purified your souls in obeying the truth through the Spirit unto unfeigned love of the brethren, see that ye love one another with a pure heart fervently.

1 Peter 1:22

Having therefore these promises, dearly beloved, let us cleanse ourselves from all filthiness of the flesh and spirit, perfecting holiness in the fear of God. 2 Corinthians 7:1

That he might sanctify and cleanse it with the washing of water by the word. Ephesians 5:26

And now, brethren, I commend you to God, and to the word of his grace, which is able to build you up, and to give you an inheritance among all them which are sanctified. Acts 20:32

FOCUSING YOUR MIND ON THE WORD OF GOD

The law of the Lord is perfect, converting the soul: the testimony of the Lord is sure, making wise the simple.

Psalms 19:7

When wisdom entereth into thine heart, and knowledge is pleasant unto thy soul. Proverbs 2:10

My son, let not them depart from thine eyes: keep sound wisdom and discretion: So shall they be life unto thy soul, and grace to thy neck. Proverbs 3:21-22

Thus saith the Lord, Stand ye in the ways, and see, and ask for the old paths, where is the good way, and walk therein, and ye shall find rest for your souls. But they said, We will not walk therein. Jeremiah 6:16

And be not conformed to this world: but be ye transformed by the renewing of your mind, that ye may prove what is that good, and acceptable, and perfect, will of God.

Romans 12:2

And be renewed in the spirit of your mind. Ephesians 4:23

This is the covenant that I will make with them after those days, saith the Lord, I will put my laws into their hearts, and in their minds will I write them. Hebrews 10:16

Wherefore lay apart all filthiness and superfluity of naughtiness, and receive with meekness the engrafted word, which is able to save your souls. James 1:21

This second epistle, beloved, I now write unto you; in both which I stir up your pure minds by way of remembrance: That ye may be mindful of the words which were spoken before by the holy prophets, and of the commandment of us the apostles of the Lord and Saviour. 2 Peter 3:1-2

For the word of God is quick, and powerful, and sharper than any twoedged sword, piercing even to the dividing asunder of soul and spirit, and of the joints and marrow, and is a discerner of the thoughts and intents of the heart.

Hebrews 4:12

OTHER PRODUCTS BY JUANITA BYNUM

BOOKS

No More Sheets - Paperback
No More Sheets - Hardback
No More Sheets - Workbook
No More Sheets - Quote Book
The Juanita Bynum Topical Bible
Don't Get Off the Train
The Planted Seed
Morning Glory - Devotional
Morning Glory - Quote Book
Morning Glory - Prayer Journal
My Inheritance - Minibook
Never Mess with a Man who Came Out of a Cave - Minibook

VIDEOS

No More Sheets
The Refiner's Fire
Resurrection Power
Tied to the Altar
The Spirit of Isaac
My Delivery

MUSIC

No More Sheets - Single (CD and Cassette)
No More Sheets - Music Video
Morning Glory - Peace (CD and Cassette)
Morning Glory - Music Video

AVAILABLE AT YOUR LOCAL BOOKSTORE OR BY CONTACTING

Juanita Bynum Ministries
Post Office Box 939
Waycross, GA 31502
800-979-9195

Pneuma Life Publishing
Post Office Box 885
Lanham, MD 20703
800-727-3218

OTHER BOOKS FROM PNEUMA LIFE PUBLISHING